Alcohol Problems

Talking with Drinkers

of related interest

Counselling – The Deaf Challenge
Marian Corker
ISBN 1 85302 223 3

Deafness and Mental Health
John C Denmark
ISBN 1 85302 212 8

Alcohol Problems

Talking with Drinkers

Gillie Ruscombe-King and Sheila Hurst
Foreword by Alex Paton, MD FRCP

Jessica Kingsley Publishers
London and Bristol, Pennsylvania

84918

First published in the United Kingdom in 1993 by
Jessica Kingsley Publishers Ltd
116 Pentonville Road
London N1 9JB

Copyright © 1993 Gillie Ruscombe-King and Sheila Hurst
Foreword Copyright © 1993 Alex Paton MD, FRCP

British Library Cataloguing in Publication Data
　　Ruscombe-King, Gillian
　　Alcohol Problems: Talking with Drinkers
　　I. Title II. Hurst, Sheila
　　362.29

　　ISBN 1 85302 206 3

Printed and Bound in Great Britain by
Cromwell Press, Melksham, Wiltshire

Contents

Acknowledgements

Many people have helped us with this book:
Our colleagues past and present with their contagious enthusiasm and
interest in alcohol problems.
Dr Rex Haigh, who began the project by us offering experience and humour;
Robert Wilson, who offered such expert editorial advice;
Rosie LeGrys, Kathy Dalley and Angela Day – who helped type and
provided great support;
Anne Gray and Pauline Stainthorp for their patient support with references;
Dr Bob Fieldsend, Dr Alex Paton and Dr Peter Sudbury,
as friends and colleagues;
our families who have supported us through all the stages of writing,
and, most important, all those who have sought our help over the years, who
have had the courage to share their difficulties
and from whom we have learnt so much.

Foreword

There is no miracle cure for severe alcohol misuse, although the occasional sudden abstention after years of chaotic drinking may seem miraculous. Claims have been made for all sorts of treatments, but most workers in the field would, I suggest, agree that counselling forms the backbone of successful management. Two ingredients are necessary: an intimate and constantly evolving knowledge of alcohol and its misuse, vital for confidence in dealing with clients; and empathy (not always the same as sympathy) on the part of the counsellor towards each individual drinker. 'True empathy', it is said, 'demands deep understanding the result of serious study'.

Counselling is a two-way interaction between client and helper (never forget that the helper too needs support). The alcohol counsellor is trained first, to understand what might be called the environment of drinking; second, to be constantly aware of his or her insight, attitudes, beliefs, prejudices and expectations; third, to be alert to the subtle clues and hidden signs of the client's drinking; and fourth, to recognise the all too common denial, anger, guilt, hostility and rationalisation of the dependent drinker.

Many health workers, including doctors, think that because of their calling, the ability to counsel is God-given. They frequently confuse advice with counselling, without stopping to think that advice is a one-way journey at the end of which the client is offered a solution which may or may not be accepted. An example might be suggesting that a heavy drinker early in his career should reduce his intake, without going into reasons for his drinking. Counselling is more like the exploration of a tropical forest where undergrowth threatens and paths lead all ways. A successful outcome depends on mutual support and understanding with a sense of purpose and direction.

As with all skills, a very few people have an instinctive penchant for counselling. The majority, however, must learn the hard way – by constant practice, by co-counselling, by attending courses like the Volunteer Alcohol Counsellors Training Scheme (VACTS), and by reading the experts. A number are available, both general and specific to alcohol, but none that I know is as comprehensive as *Alcohol Problems: Talking with Drinkers*. It is clearly divided into two parts: the background knowledge required to understand why people drink to excess, and a series of dialogues illustrating ways to deal with the many problems presented by drinkers. Considering the difficulties of conveying the complexities of human behaviour, it is written in a style which will commend it not only to all health and social workers involved in alcohol misuse but also to drinkers and their families who wish to understand what makes people drink to excess. I wonder if the authors realise how much of their own compassion comes through in this outstandingly sympathetic book.

Alex Paton MD, FRCP

Introduction

'All along, the present takes its texture from portions of the past that are hinted at or revealed'.

'And all along we realise that this special day – special because it is the day that Ed learns that he has TB and Mary returns to her addiction – is really like every other day in the rounds of accusation and regret, hate and love that make up the family experience'.

(from *Long Day's Journey into Night* – Eugene O'Neill)

Inspiration for this book arose from talking to many people – to those who drink and to those who do not drink; to those who have contact both personally and professionally with a family experience not dissimilar from that so vividly described by Eugene O'Neill.

We recognised that so often the experiences of the families involved with drinkers were parallelled by our own experiences as 'professionals'. The helplessness often felt by the families was shared, at times, by those 'helping' and by the drinkers themselves. This commonality draws the helper, the drinker and the family into an alliance which can be enabling. Or the alliance can become paralysing and disabling. The chapters in this book draw on examples which illustrate this idea.

Although drinking problems pose enormous challenges, the expertise to tackle them can be found within us all and we believe that the major task in tackling alcohol misuse is to help find that expertise. We would like to convey the sense that all helpers and drinkers can believe in their own abilities to rise to this challenge. Intervention is necessary when confidence and belief in that personal ability is lost and this can happen to all.

Throughout this book, the term 'drinker' is used to describe the person who is using/abusing alcohol as his or her way of dealing with conflict. We use this term because notions of 'the alcoholic' or 'the heavy drinker' carry connotations and societal prejudice. Such labels can impede understanding of the nature of the problem and can alienate the drinker struggling to cope with the difficulties that arise from his or her drinking. The 'drinker' may be you, or us, or my neighbour or our children's teacher, or the local milkman or... Alcohol misuse has no barriers. We have therefore used the term 'drinker' to avoid dividing the population into 'them' and 'us'.

In recent years, we have come to understand drinking in terms of a psychological and/or physical addiction which leaves the drinker vulnerable to the use or misuse of alcohol when under stress. Since in this book we shall explore how the addiction may take hold, the scope of the term 'drinker' has been widened so that we also talk to moderate drinkers who are some way along the path to a potential addiction. Drinking behaviour can be seen on a continuum and the 'drinker' has to decide where he or she is along that path.

Both men and women can be drinkers. Both men and women can meet with drinkers. In order to embrace this, he/she can be read, in the text, as interchangeable, except where there is clear indication for clarification.

The book is divided into two sections: the first five chapters outline a theoretical basis for understanding the nature of drinking problems and why they may arise, and include information about the medical consequences of heavy drinking. These are followed by dialogue chapters, written in dialogue form to sustain the notion of the encounter *in vivo* between those that are or have been drinking and those that meet them. The term 'talker' is used in this section to describe the person who is 'listening' and responding to the drinker. That person can come from any walk of life.

The 'dialogue' chapters encourage the reader to explore points raised from both sides of the dialogue. Through the use of process notes accompanying the conversations, there is an opportunity to clarify and disentangle some of the misunderstandings that can take place. Some theoretical perspectives are offered in the 'theory' chapters. The contents of the conversations represent the collective experience of the authors and their colleagues, gained from talking with their clients.

Theories about the causes of heavy drinking are abundant, complex and at times appear contradictory. While wishing to recognise the contributions of the many different theories about the origins of alcohol abuse, the theoretical framework outlined, particularly in Chapter 3, is one that is advanced and fruitfully used in clinical practise by us, the authors. We do not pretend or claim to have the answers.

Sheila Hurst
Gillie Ruscombe-King

CHAPTER 1

'I'm Just a Social Drinker!'

Definitions and Consequences of Drinking Behaviour

Drinking in moderation carries few risks for most people. It has the effect of making us feel good: more confident, joyful, with a sense of well being. For some, whose drinking is heavy, out of control and financially crippling, the picture is somewhat different.

Imagine the scene: in which

a	husband		
	friend		'You think I'm an alcoholic, don't
	wife	says	you. Well, I may be drinking,
	son		but it's not a problem to me.
	father		You're the one who is
	daughter		complaining.'
	colleague		
and the	father		
	daughter		
	colleague		
	son	replies	'but you are causing so much
	friend		worry.'
	husband		
	wife		

This short interchange suggests some of the issues that are created by the use and abuse of alcohol. In the interchange, the drinker sees little of the concern or damage that the drinking is causing to self and others. When discussion arises, the problem is externalised. Thus ownership of the problem is batted between the speakers, when really both face a problem but from differing positions.

These issues have to be faced by individuals, families, employers, everyone in our society. Alcohol is a drug that has been used by man for centuries. When consumed, it may create either sadness or joy, excitement or despair; generosity and hospitality, or destitution and isolation; pride and confidence, or anxiety and low self-esteem; it can be life enriching and it can cause death. Alcohol poses a paradox that has to be faced by individuals, by professionals and by society at large.

The particular and unique property of alcohol is that it creates simultaneously a shift in mood and a shift in how that mood is perceived. That is why it is used. And it is this shift in perception that can embroil us all – drinkers, non-drinkers, professionals, clients, politicians, children. In this chapter we hope to clarify some of the social, psychological and medical factors that are the consequences of the use and abuse of alcohol, and to look at some definitions on which to base our own understanding and perceptions.

Alcohol is a drug that acts as a depressant on the central nervous system. It is absorbed directly from the stomach into the bloodstream. As the absorption rate is fast, the effects on the brain physiology are almost immediate after ingestion. The shaking or agitated drinker is quickly calmed by the 'first' of the day. Its depressant qualities will act first on those areas of the brain that have, in man, evolved last. Social inhibition, emotional tension, social restraints are reduced first as if a dam is slowly being opened.

With the very first drink, there is a loss of clarity, with reduced understanding about the drinker's change of functioning. At the same time there is a surge of confidence and a sense of well being. The rapidity with which these changes take place is indicated by studies of drinking and driving which suggest that, after only one drink, you are four times more likely to have an accident. Alcohol increases the risk of an accident by reducing co-ordination of movement, slowing reaction time, blurring vision, decreasing awareness, impairing ability to judge speed and distances and giving a false sense of confidence in performing skilled tasks (Royal College of Physicians 1987:82).

On the other hand, as loss of social inhibition takes place, greater bonhomie, generosity and excitement lead to many of us 'having a good time'. Confidence and gaiety are increased and social performance becomes successful, interesting and worthwhile. So, in spite of the fact that, with increased consumption, concentration is lost, speech becomes slurred and for some, the 'good time' does not last long, drinking is valued by many of us. Dealing with the issues surrounding drinking is therefore complex and produces an ambivalent response.

This ambivalence towards alcohol is reflected in the overall attitude of society. Statistics convey a frightening picture of the impact of alcohol on our community. In 1990, in Great Britain, 28 per cent of men drink more than the medically recommended sensible limit of 21 units per week and 11 per cent of women drink more than the medically recommended limit of 14 units (General Household Survey 1990) and as many as 500 young people die annually from accidents related to drunkenness.

This represents 10 per cent of all deaths under 25 years of age (Sabey and Coding 1975). In the US as many as 80 per cent of cases of family violence involve alcohol (Jacob and Seilhamer 1982). Yet, in spite of these statistics, alcohol, unlike other drugs that are seen to cause harm, is not outlawed.

That alcohol as a drug can, at least temporarily, create a shift towards well-being suggests, perhaps, why it is so universally used. Man has consistently and creatively searched for altered feelings – through trance, meditation and drugs. Drinking alcohol has become the most socially acceptable way of achieving this much sought after experience. Conversely, what makes drinking uncomfortable for the tee-totaller can be the fear of a perceptual and emotional shift.

Terms and Definitions

Measures

Alcohol consumption is normally described in terms of numbers of pints or bottles, depending on what is being drunk. More specifically, a standard drink from a public house measure can be broken down into grammes of alcohol, more easily translated into 'units'. For example:

Half pint of beer
One glass of table wine =   One unit *or* 8 grammes of alcohol
One glass of sherry
One single whisky

It has been estimated that men who drink 21 units per week or less, (that is ten and a half pints of beer or 21 glasses of wine for the whole week) with one or two days without alcohol, will have minimal risk of harm to themselves or their family. For women, the limit is lower. More than 14 units per week, (that is, seven pints of beer or 14 glasses of wine) increases the risk of harm to themselves and to those around them. Because alcohol is carried in the bloodstream and may reach the foetus, pregnant women are advised to abstain or have no more than 1–2 units, (one pint of beer or one to two glasses of wine) once or twice a week.

We will all know people who can drink at these levels, seemingly without severe problems. The alcohol consumption of many readers of this book may be higher than, or close to the recommended limits. Consumption of alcohol in the UK has risen from 4.4 litres in 1960 to 7.2 litres in 1991 (The Brewer's Society). Few people can escape the immediate psychological consequences of drinking alcohol. The altered perceptual and emotional state creates denial: 'Oh I'll just have another one, it can't do me any harm'. 'I am quite all right to drive home'. And many of us may have experienced the wrestle between the rational understanding of the effect of alcohol and the desire to take the risk. However, once the drink is taken, alcohol reduces the dilemma. The consequences can be forgotten or seen to be ascribed to the 'overt' drinker. 'Alcoholics sit on park benches'. 'There goes Bert, it must be opening time!'

Patterns of drinking

Patterns of drinking vary enormously between individuals. Binge drinking, secret drinking, pub drinking, drinking behind closed doors, 'I never touch a drop till 6.00' drinking, non-stop drinking describe just a few. The pattern and type of drinking may well be an indication of the origins of the individual's problems, as a demonstration and communication of the distress. It may be a pointer to sociability, shyness, marital and family disharmony, background, expectations of alcohol and cultural forces. But most important, it may suggest why alcohol is needed. For example, a woman picks up a drink at 6.00 p.m. repeatedly. What is the alcohol for? Societal expectations may say that is quite acceptable. Physiologically she does not need the alcohol (to start with, anyway). Perhaps it is saying more about what is happening or not happening for her at that time of day.

Publicly, the world sees the gross extremes of drinking patterns – the 'after a session' scenario when an individual may be highly intoxicated; the street drinkers who seem to be at it all the time. Any pattern of drinking can be adapted to individual lifestyles in a very sophisticated way – the wife who remains in the dark for years about her husband's secret drinking; the businessman who maintains a demanding high powered job with a consistently high blood alcohol level. It is often when the sophisticated pattern is unexpectedly interrupted, through, for example a car crash, that the real extent of the drinking is revealed (see Chapter 9, dialogue 2).

Binge or 'bout' drinking, when drinking has a clearly defined limit of time – the all or nothing – can be bewildering to drinkers, helpers and families. 'If she can stop now, why can't she stay stopped?'. Perhaps, on closer inquiry, the situation may not be so clear cut. The periods of abstinence may be an attempt to grab at stopping a pattern of continuous heavy drinking, which can only be maintained for a limited period of time. Pressures mount, tensions increase. Most people experience mood swings, be they fleeting moments or long periods of depression. The bout drinker is manifesting mood swings by using alcohol.

As a result, there remains a continuing debate about who is a social/heavy/ abusive drinker. 'It's all right, I am just a heavy drinker.' In 1987, the Royal College of Physicians (1987) gave the following definitions:

> **Social Drinker** – Someone who drinks usually not more than two to three units (one pint of beer or two to three glasses of wine) of alcohol a day and does not become intoxicated. The amount that can be drunk without harm varies widely between individuals, but greater amounts than this are associated with increasing risk of harm.
>
> **Heavy drinker** – Someone who regularly drinks more than six units (three pints of beer or six glasses of wine) of alcohol a day but without apparent immediate harm.

Problem drinker – Someone who experiences physical, psychological, social, family, occupational, financial or legal problems attributable to drinking.

Dependent drinker – Someone who has a compulsion to drink; takes roughly the same amount each day; has increased tolerance to alcohol in the early stages and reduced tolerance later; suffers withdrawal symptoms if alcohol is stopped which are relieved by consuming more; in whom drinking takes precedence over other activities and who tends to resume drinking after a period of abstinence.

They do stress in the report that these divisions are arbitrary, that social drinking may tip into heavy drinking and that some who drink a little may experience greater problems than some who drink more. As an indication of the relative numbers of different sorts of drinkers, it has been estimated that a general practitioner with 2,000 patients on his list would have 135 heavy drinkers, forty problem drinkers and seven alcohol-dependent patients on his or her list (Anderson 1983).

Furthermore, the way people drink also affects the harm which may occur. If an individual drinks all the week's units of alcohol on one night, he may get 'blind drunk' and become involved in a fight, petty crime or conflict in a relationship, causing some considerable disruption to his and others' well being. Each person's emotional and physiological interaction with alcohol will be an individual process and the capacity for individual variation is enormous.

'Alcoholic' and 'Alcoholism?'

In the report of the Royal College of Physicians, the view is that the terms 'alcoholic' and 'alcoholism', though widely used, are impossible to define. They are not used in the report 'because they carry with them the mistaken idea that the condition is irrevocable and untreatable' (Royal College of Physicians 1987 p.5). We agree that such a view of alcoholism is wholly inappropriate. Alcoholism is commonly, but mistakenly, seen as the end of the road. However, it is our experience that it is sometimes only at the point where the notion of 'alcoholism' as opposed to 'dependent drinking' is openly discussed that the real severity and nature of the problem is entertained and addressed. The denial, described briefly above, begins to be countered. The penny drops – for some with great shock, for others with considerable relief.

The word, or notion, 'alcoholism' creates enormous ripples of embarrassment, discomfort, disbelief, rage, and sadness for the drinker, and carries connotations for the professional, sister, husband, employer, or child, of social stigma, unemployment, or destitution. But it is to embrace these very issues that the notion can, and at times must be used, with accuracy and sensitivity. It is not the hangman's noose. Avoidance of the issue perpetuates the social stereotype, condemns those who have the courage to declare their problems openly and, most important, colludes with the principle psychological and physiological process of the drug alcohol – the perceptual shift towards denial. For these reasons, from time to time in this book we use the term 'alcoholic' as synonymous with 'dependent drinker', especially in the dialogue chapters (see Chapter. 6–11).

Consequences of Heavy Drinking

Social problems

The drug alcohol reduces inhibition, leading to talkativeness, excitement. As the limits get overstepped, discussion can lead to argument, perhaps to violence and even violent crime. The social consequences of heavy drinking are manifold. It is estimated that the lives of 15 people are directly and significantly affected by the behaviour of one dependent drinker. After a 'heavy' night, any drinker may feel irritable and grumpy, argue with the spouse, smack the children needlessly, be late for work, concentrate badly, make poor decisions, come home recklessly and turn to the bottle to calm down. Further along the drinking continuum, the argument with the spouse leads to violence towards her and the children; he gets to work to be given notice; on the way home he crashes the car and kills an innocent bystander.

Clearly, the interaction between the individual, the family and societal influences is very complex and no one aspect can be seen in isolation. It is, however, acknowledged that alcohol intoxication has significant impact on every aspect of this complexity.

FAMILY

Tensions created in the family by unpredictable intoxication can become extreme, for the drinker and non drinker alike, no matter which member of the family is drinking. Fear, despair, guilt, loneliness, hopelessness, confusion, anger are a few of the wide range of feelings which may be experienced within the family setting. A third of problem drinkers quote marital discord as one of their problems (Jacob and Seilhamer 1982). With intoxication, responsibilities are shed, and inevitably embraced by another member of the family – sister, eldest child, spouse. With a heavy drinking adolescent, or unpartnered drinking man, the toll commonly 'falls' on the mother. It is often the exhaustion caused by constantly changing emotional arousal in the face of uncertainty and unpredictability that becomes so defeating for family members. Sleeplessness, depression and even attempted suicide can result.

For the children, bewilderment and fear is ever present. One minute Dad gives them a sweet, the next minute a hiding. Social anxiety can prevail, interrupting the formation of good peer relationships. They can become socially isolated as they are too scared to bring friends home. Feelings of acute disappointment and loss of trust result as mum's drinking once again prevents her from meeting the school bus. These examples appear to be extreme, but such anxieties can be aroused at any level of drinking. Preoccupation about home can disturb concentration, leading to poor school performance and the need for special input – more humiliation.

Witnessing unexpressed resentments, or constant arguments with the risk of pending parental separation, will inevitably take its toll. The need to make alliances with one or other party for security can destructively backfire as resentments are taken out on the children. Overt behavioural disturbances may result. And the risk of physical injury with the enormous implications which that carries for any child can never be discounted.

As the children grow older, they may spend less and less time at home and more time with others who feel equally disaffected, and so may start drinking or drug taking. They may soon become strong enough to fight back, escalating the potential for violence and injury. Or they may remain nervously at home, in protection of a parent or other siblings, trying to maintain some control, missing valuable years of development and exploration. Anorexia can often creep into the picture. There is little exact evidence of the effects of children growing up with a heavy drinking parent but any parent is providing a model for the child to learn by. If that model is unpredictable, the world, at the very least, is confusing. There is more discussion of this issue in Chapter 3.

DRINKING IN OLD AGE

Granny Jones, with her daily bottle of sherry is often dismissed as 'a bit eccentric', with statements such as 'let her be, it's all she has left'. Yet drinking in old age can cause untold misery for those burdened with the responsibility for the elderly person. Risk of self harm, injury through falls and risk to self and others by fire cannot so easily be discounted. The effects of alcohol on an already frail system will increase the likelihood of irritable, unreasonable and demanding behaviour, forgetfulness and unsteadiness of limbs, creating a dilemma for family, friends and professionals over whether such an individual can remain responsible for his/her own decisions. Management of such dilemmas can present huge problems, as illustrated in Chapter 11, dialogue 1.

Economic problems

The British spend more on alcohol than they do on clothes, cars hospitals, schools or universities (Saunders 1984). Such a statistic says much about the priority given to alcohol in the majority of people's lives. To fund the habit of continual alcohol consumption will take a large chunk out of a 'normal' family's income – money otherwise needed for shoes, school outings, in some cases even food. For the young single person, 'free of responsibility', there is often great regret at the wasted money or friendships broken through constant borrowing. Debt is a very common hazard associated with heavy alcohol consumption. It creates tensions, resentments, misery, even bankruptcy; it can contribute to family break-up and homelessness. Debt can lead to crime – petty theft to subsidise the habit of drinking, burglary to reclaim spent resources, begging and violence in attempts to gain desperately needed funds.

EMPLOYMENT

It is generally recognised that most problem drinkers are in full time, gainful employment and that alcohol problems can occur at any strata of the working community, from the very top right through to those in less demanding occupations. Alcohol has no barriers. With heavy consumption, concentration diminishes, work performance decreases, the likelihood of accidents and danger to others increases; attendance slips, promotion is lost, and redundancy or dismissal is possible. Unemployment can result, which increases economic hardship, and it may be very difficult to rejoin the work place.

From the national point of view, the cost to industry of heavy drinking is substantial. The Royal College of Physicians (1987 p.9) cite the following as contributory:

1. Sickness absence.

2. Unexplained absence from the job and lateness to work.

3. Reduced efficiency and decision making at work.

4. Impaired industrial relations.

5. Early retirement and premature death.

6. Higher labour turnover and retraining.

Crime

DRIVING

It is estimated by the Home Office that only one in two hundred and fifty episodes of driving when over the legal limit for blood alcohol level of 80 mg/per 100ml results in police intervention leading to conviction (Riley 1984). This is likely to be a conservative estimate but this level of drinking and driving creates great danger for all road users: drivers, passengers, cyclists or pedestrians.

OTHER OFFENCES

Alcohol disinhibits and is closely associated with crimes of theft, violence and mob riot. Of 121 British offenders serving sentences for burglary, about one third said their offences were usually committed under the influence of alcohol (Bennett and Wright 1984). In the West of Scotland, more than half of 400 people found guilty of homicide were intoxicated when they committed the murder. And, more than half their victims were also intoxicated (Gillies 1976). Petty theft, fraud, embezzlement, begging – all commonly occur as a response to the need for money to continue the habit of drinking.

Behind the veil of unreported crimes of child assault, domestic violence and private and public affray lie tales of untold misery and huge personal hardship. Loyalty and fear can overwhelm anger and revenge. 'I know he beats me up but I do love him.'

Accidents and injuries

'Alcohol Abuse is the single most important factor contributing to bodily damage and adds considerably to the severity of the injuries that may be sustained' (Royal College of Physicians 1987). As stated earlier, the greatest risk of alcohol related injuries is from road traffic accidents. The statistics prove depressing reading. At the Birmingham Accident Hospital in England, one survey suggested that 40 percent of victims of road accidents had been drinking (White 1980).

Pedestrians walking home while intoxicated cause injury to themselves by falling and risk of injury to others by falling onto another pedestrian, or in the path of a passing vehicle, causing the driver to swerve. In those that have become intoxicated, falls in the home contribute significantly to the number of injuries seen, as do injuries and deaths from fire and drowning. Thirty per cent of persons who take their own lives are excessive drinkers and alcohol is involved in 60 per cent of attempted suicides (Platt 1983). Injury to others will vary from a broken nose in a drunken brawl, to the black eye of a loved family member, and to the impulsive attack of a comparative stranger. Some injuries are more commonly associated with acute intoxication than with chronic abuse. This is especially the case in homicide and child abuse.

The personal cost is huge; the national cost is also enormous. Police, courts, probation service, ambulances, social services, general hospitals, GPs, lawyers, health visitors, firemen, psychiatrists can all be involved with one single domestic affray.

Homelessness and vagrancy

The sight of a park bench drinker with his grubby clothes and unshaven appearance is often held as 'typical' of how alcohol can ruin an individual. And it has to be said that alcohol has in many cases contributed to his circumstances. Of 158 men in a homeless mens hostel in Sweden, 145 exhibited signs of alcohol dependence (Borg 1978). Equally, the drinkers describe the disintegration of family life from an early age, or a series of traumatic life events spiralling them into the rootless, chaotic lifestyle, which paradoxically, alongside alcohol, becomes their main system of support and friendship (see Chapter 11 dialogue 2).

The Personal Costs of Heavy Drinking

Psychological consequences

Let's return to the opening scenario of this chapter:

> 'Well, I may be drinking, but it is not a problem for me. You're the one who is complaining'.

The unspoken thoughts and feelings behind these words are legion and point to some of the psychological suffering the drinker bears. Feelings of guilt, sadness, confusion, disbelief, anxiety, and isolation are acute. When alcohol is consumed, a perceptual shift is experienced which may be described, in emotional terms, as one of denial. There is then a rational and intellectual response to the loss of emotional clarity, followed by persuasiveness, perhaps arrogance, to complete the cover-up. And so the psychological spiral is set up.

With increased consumption, these 'defences' become entrenched in the personality structure of the individual and access to the original sensitivities and emotionality is temporarily lost. Personality changes seem to take place and some drinkers are referred to as if they are acting uncharacteristically. 'Oh she is so soppy when she has had a drink'. 'He's just a Jekyll and Hyde. He is a different person when he's drinking'.

In all of us, emotional aspects and inner anxieties can be suppressed by psychological defences. Alcohol depresses those defences, enabling expression of the buried personality. However, the turmoil caused by such expression can be great, and as protection from the turmoil of the external world, and relief from the stress of inner anxieties, the drinker continues to drink. And so the vicious cycle of psychological dependency is created. This subject is discussed in greater detail in Chapters 3 and 4.

Medical consequences

DIGESTION AND METABOLISM

When talking about alcohol to drink, we refer to ethyl alcohol, which is made up of carbon, hydrogen and oxygen in a simple combination to form a colourless fluid. Alcohol is made from fermentation by yeasts of sugars that occur naturally in plants – beer from barley, cider from apples, wine from grapes. When consumed, alcohol creates an effect on the lining of the mouth, the oesophagus, the stomach and the upper part of the intestine.

The food value of an alcoholic drink is significant because of the sugar used in its manufacture. It is a carbohydrate and because of its quick absorption from the stomach, it provides energy instantly. Therefore, it can replace and depress a natural appetite. However, the energy created cannot be used effectively by the body because of the uncoordinating effects of the drug, and it cannot, therefore, be used to supplement a diet. Indeed, in the long term, it can completely erode a natural hunger.

Alcohol affects the action of the nervous system by reducing its activity, through the depressant nature of the drug. As suggested earlier, for many it appears to be a stimulant – the timid become bolder, the placid more assertive. The action of the alcohol depresses first those aspects of human mental activity that have evolutionary formed last. Social inhibition is the first to be affected and, as consumption increases, further aspects of mental functioning become temporarily impaired until the individual is 'legless' or even comatose. It will be all too apparent that neurological activity is disrupted by continual heavy consumption.

How two different individuals respond to the one drug alcohol and, indeed, to the same amount may vary enormously and will depend on their own metabolic processes and psychological responses to its effects. An average man could be over the legal drink/drive limit of 80mg/100ml by drinking as little as two pints of ordinary strength beer (four units) or its equivalent in other drinks. Similarly, a woman could be over the legal limit after one and a half pints beer or three units. This depends on the rate at which absorption into the blood stream takes place in that individual. Some people have more tolerance, can 'hold their drink'. Some are instantly irritated by its presence in their systems.

Some can increase their tolerance so different parts of the body become used to having alcohol in its tissues, and can continue to function while adapting to the presence of alcohol in ever increasing amounts. This is especially true of the brain, and may explain why some remarkably heavy consumption can go unnoticed for a considerable length of time. However, in an individual with a long drinking career, tolerance may suddenly decline, so that they become intoxicated on the smallest amounts and, tremulous and agitated, vomit the very poison that has been so faithful in the past.

The rate at which alcohol is oxidised (broken down) in the body does not alter and is not affected by the concentration of alcohol in the system. It takes much longer for a heavy consumer to reduce the amount of alcohol in his system than it takes a moderate drinker. Four pints of beer (or eight units) will take four to five hours to be oxidised. Twice that amount will take twice as long. Because of this, people who drink slowly but continually take as long to recover as those who have absorbed the same amount rapidly.

Alcohol is absorbed directly from the stomach and goes quickly into body tissue and fluid. Its destruction, by oxidation, takes place mainly in the liver where it is broken down into carbon dioxide and water. A small quantity, about 2 per cent , is excreted in the urine and in the breath. The amount of alcohol exhaled is very small, yet is enough to detect the concentration of alcohol in the blood through the use of breath tests. The smell on a drinker's breath is caused by other components of the 'drink' and does not clearly indicate the extent of intoxication.

Physiological dependence

With habitual and heavy consumption, physiological processes take place which contribute to the difficulty in stopping drinking. Alcohol calms and depresses. Without the quantity of alcohol that the body has become accustomed to, psychological and physical craving emerges and the individual can feel agitated, anxious, even panicky.

Physiologically, the same process occurs. A clear sign of a reduction of alcohol in the bloodstream is agitation, internal 'butterflies', tremulousness of the hands, commonly known as 'the shakes'. These signs are especially observable in the mornings, as during a night's sleep, the alcohol/blood level will drop, unless the drinker wakes in the night for a drink. The agitation leads to sleeplessness. Alcohol at these levels distorts the natural sleep pattern.

Irregular meals and a poor diet, absorbed through an inflamed stomach lining due to irritation from alcohol, contributes to nausea, morning vomiting and leads on to gastritis, weakness and malnutrition, which is seen as one of the most serious medical consequences of chronic alcohol abuse. Alcohol provides carbohydrates but lacks vitamins, especially vitamin B. Through lack of food, the body cannot begin to repair the assaulted stomach and liver, and as further anorexia continues, the nutritional deficiencies themselves contribute to cirrhosis, the formation of stomach ulcers and chronic gastritis. The brain, too, will become affected.

Listed below is what can happen to the drinker as a result of physiological dependence.

SIGNS OF DEPENDENT DRINKING

1. **Narrowing of Repertoire**	External events may no longer dictate volume of consumption. Drinking becomes associated with relief or avoidance of withdrawal. Pattern of drinking and type of drink becomes fixed.
2. **Drinking becomes a priority**	Less time spent with hobbies, family, responsibilities, and more time and priority to drinking, even in the face of health hazards – 'I'd rather go down happy'.
3. **Increased tolerance to alcohol**	Sustained increased tolerance to alcohol, which may incapacitate the non-tolerant drinker, but allows the individual to go about his business. In later stages, the tolerance can suddenly change and the drinker may become very drunk on previously 'tolerated' amounts.
4. **Onset of physical dependency**	Heavy drinkers may become physically dependent on alcohol. In other words, their bodies are unable to function normally without alcohol, when consumption ceases.

Symptoms may appear 24 hours after stopping drinking and last for a period of one to five days. Each individual's response is different and it is impossible to predict which and in which order symptoms may appear. There may be no symptoms; there may be a combination.

ACUTE SIGNS OF PHYSIOLOGICAL DEPENDENCY

Withdrawal symptoms	Agitation, tremulousness, butterflies, shaking hands, jumpiness, easy distraction. Response to lack of 'calming' effect of alcohol. Brain is no longer 'depressed' and becomes overstimulated, especially when blood alcohol level is reduced.
Sweating	Often reported at night, waking with drenched sheets. Sweaty palms and face as if body is in flight.

Nausea and morning vomiting.	
Anorexia	Loss of appetite.
Sleeplessness	Caused by agitation and general restlessness by reduced blood alcohol level. Sleep pattern disturbed by alcohol.
Epileptic fits	Due to sudden and sharp reduction of alcohol in the brain, prompting unexpected and frightening seizures. One of the many reasons why reduction or withdrawal from alcohol needs to be carefully monitored.
Hallucinations	Usually short-lived, described as a vivid nightmare that is difficult to untangle from reality. May be visual or auditory. Things may appear distorted in shape. May be accompanied by restlessness, disorientation and poor concentration.
Delirium Tremens or 'DTs'	Extreme fear, bewilderment and chaotic thinking due to complete disorganisation of the brain. Disorientation. Hallucinations are very vivid, commonly visual. Can begin two to five days after cessation of drinking, after some ten years of heavy consumption. Occurrence rare.

Long Term Medical Consequences of Heavy Drinking

1. Intestinal problems

Gastritis	The lining of the stomach becomes inflamed by the direct irritant properties of alcohol, especially strong drinks, for example spirits. The stomach wall becomes covered in mucus.
Ulcers	Exacerbated and irritated by alcohol. Duodenal and peptic. Bleeding may occur.
Pancreatitis	Causing severe pain in the back or abdomen.
2. Malnutrition	Poor absorption and continual anorexia leads to a cycle of poor nourishment.
3. Liver disease	The alcohol itself exerts a direct toxic effect on the liver cells, and, coupled with poor absorption of food from the intestine and low vitamins from an inadequate diet prevents the liver from ever repairing itself. In the early stages, damage to the liver may be mild and reversible. As the disease progresses, the cells become hardened and scarred

(cirrhosis) with symptoms of anorexia, flatulence and jaundice. If drinking stops, the healthy non cirrhotic parts of the liver can regenerate.

4. Neurological problems

Black outs and alcoholic amnesias

Loss of memory can be a common feature of heavy drinking, but loss of any recall of events suggests considerable interference with brain functioning.

Peripheral neuritis 'pins and needles'

Caused by lack of vitamins as a consequence of malnutrition. The long nerves to the hands and feet are affected, giving a tingling feeling. Sensory nerves are affected first, hence walking is cautious and uncertain. Recovery can be complete with increased vitamin B.

Wernicke-Korsackoff Syndrome Wernicke's encephalopathy

Acute type of memory loss with slowness in answering, difficulty in concentration and associated neurological signs. Can be averted with intense vitamin treatment, but once present, is hard to retrieve.

Korsakoff's Psychosis

Again, caused by vitamin deficiency. A disorder of memory where recent events are lost, whereas events from the past are remembered quite well. Those affected seem clear headed, articulate and reasonable but after some dialogue it becomes clear there is no retention of recent events and what is happening around them. To compensate, they may confabulate; they seem to able to converse, but the content of their conversation is hollow and inconsistent. This condition is incurable.

Alcoholic Dementia

Memory loss and intellectual impairment. Caused by the destruction of the brain cells. Can be intercepted if drinking stops, but once present, is irreversible.

5. Psychological disorders

Pathological jealousy

Uncertain whether heavy drinking creates the jealous thoughts or whether the drinking is used to try and quell the unpleasant thoughts. Mainly affecting men, directed towards their female partners with an expression of jealousy of much greater intensity than normal. Will lessen if drinking stops.

Alcoholic Hallucinosis	Not common. Hearing voices referring to person concerned. In few cases, can persist when drinking stops. Different in essence to the disorganised visual sensations of DTs.

Clearly, some individuals will experience a variety of physical symptoms, varying in intensity and severity. Others will experience little in the way of physical discomfort. It is impossible to predict how any individual is going to react when drinking stops, but it is always wise to be cautious because of the potential severity of the symptoms. Likewise, if an individual does not experience 'nasty' symptoms, it does not mean that her drinking is any more or less under control, or even any less harmful. It may just be easier to sweep it under the carpet. The amount of alcohol consumed in a specific time is the key issue.

To return to the statements made at the beginning of this chapter:

Drinker   'You think I'm an alcoholic, don't you? Well, I may be drinking, but it is not a problem to me. You are the one who is complaining'.

Talker   'but you are causing so much worry'.

the dialogue may continue:

Drinker   'So what! Jo, down the pub, drinks twice as much as me.

Talker   'But what about the mortgage!'

and so on...

The sentiments are familiar, even identifiable. In spite of the social, personal and financial consequences, the heavy drinking may continue until such time as a clear understanding of the complexities of a drinking problem can be grasped and individually addressed.

CHAPTER 2

'Why Me?'

Contributing Factors

Many people, when faced with a drinking problem, for themselves or for others, ask the question 'Why me?' or 'Why my father?' This is sometimes said through self-pity, but more commonly because of sheer bewilderment and confusion in the drinker and in those around him. To add to the confusion, there is no clear or simple answer, as the factors that contribute to an alcohol problem are numerous, complex and all interrelated. They will be highlighted in this chapter. There is no single cause that can explain why some become dependent on alcohol, or even what promotes a liking or dislike for drink (see Figure 1).

Constitutional Factors

Various theories are put forward to explain the interaction between the drug alcohol and the physical constitution of the individual drinker. In Alcoholics Anonymous, there is a belief that, in 'alcoholics', there is an allergic factor at work which, for those affected, creates a craving for alcohol and a dependence on it. This theory of allergy has little support from the medical profession, as no evidence has been found to support it.

Another theory suggests that those who become heavily physically dependent on alcohol have been born with an enzyme abnormality which increases the need for certain substances in the body (Kessel and Walton 1989). This sets up a metabolic pattern that makes a physical addiction to alcohol more likely. This theory has not been proven. No research has yet demonstrated the existence of an enzyme abnormality. Other theories have sought to suggest alternative physiological complications, by looking at dietary levels and acetaldehyde levels, but again nothing conclusive has emerged. The complication in looking for a physical cause of heavy drinking is that metabolic changes take place in the body as soon as the alcohol is ingested. Without a chance to study an individual's constitutional make up prior to drinking, it has proved to be virtually impossible to make a comparison after drinking has started.

The Drug Alcohol

Constitution
Metabolic
Genetic

Availability	Allergic	**Personality**
Price	Dietary.	Learned Behaviour
Occupation		Predisposed
Social Acceptability		personality
Cultural Factors.		Anxiety/Stress
		reduction
		Psychodynamic
		influences.

Social Factors
Early environment
Parental drinking
Models
Peer pressure.

Figure 1: Causes of heavy drinking patterns

Hereditary Factors

Some people ask if alcohol dependence can be inherited. Looking at figure 1, it is clear that the answer is not straightforward. It is known that the sons of heavy drinking fathers have a much higher likelihood of being heavy drinkers than other men of their age. The daughters of heavy drinking mothers are equally at risk (Hore 1976). So is the propensity to heavy drinking inherited through the genes, is it a result of copied behaviour, or is it influenced by cultural and familial expectations? There are no certain answers. Not very much is yet known about the way that personality is genetically determined, and not enough to be clear how or indeed whether an 'alcoholic' factor is passed on within the personality.

However, since the late 19th century alcohol problems have been seen to run in families. Whilst there have been studies arguing from psychoanalytical evidence (Menninger 1938, McCord and McCord 1960) that alcohol problems could not be inherited, in more recent years there have been studies which provide evidence to allow Goodwin to state that genetic factors play a signifi-cant role (Goodwin 1979). He began an adoption study in 1970 interviewing the sons of Danish alcoholics raised by non-biological adoptive parents and a group of sons raised by their own alcoholic, biological parents. They were paired with a control group without alcoholic parents matched for age with the adopted group. He found that the men whose biological parents were alcoholic were four times more likely to have severe alcohol problems than were the sons of non alcoholic biological parents, irrespective of whether they had been adopted.

Goodwin also found that there was not a significant relationship between alcohol abuse in adoptees and the presence or absence of alcohol abuse in their adoptive parents. Cadoret, Cain and Grove's (1980) study showed that psychiatric and alcohol problems in adopting families did not determine alcoholism in biologically unrelated adoptees.

Whilst these studies stand, Merikanges (1990) argues that there is still some difficulty in identifying the specific genetic component of alcoholism. He points to the notion already suggested that, in addition to a possible genetic explanation for the strong degree of familial aggregation of alcohol problems, alternative explanations need to be further evaluated. They include: modelling of parental behaviour; possible changes in the susceptibility of the foetus to alcohol as a result of maternal ingestion of alcohol; results of negligent rearing manifested by dietary deficiency; exposure to brain trauma or damage to paternal sperm cells.

It is obviously very difficult to separate the environmental impact of those relatives that abuse alcohol from their genetic contribution. However, in a long and clearly documented study undertaken by Vaillant (1983), it was significant that when just the effect of alcohol abuse in ancestors (that is, in relatives who were not also part of the subject's environment) was examined, men with several alcohol abusing ancestors were twice as likely (29%) to become alcohol dependent as were men (14%) with no known alcohol-abusing ancestors.

However, Mendleson and Mello (1979) assert that 'it is unlikely that individual and racial differences in alcohol metabolism can account for alcohol abuse'. Studies show that diverse Mongolian populations including the Chinese, who have low rates of alcohol abuse and Native American subgroups, who have a notoriously high rate of alcohol abuse, share the same inborn metabolic intolerance to alcohol and its metabolites. And Utne et al. (1977) who have observed that genetic factors control the rate of metabolism of alcohol, also point out that the elimination rate of alcohol does not differ in those children who have alcoholic or non alcoholic parents. Kessel and Walton would go as far as to say that, 'while there may be some genetic transmission of alcoholism, the non-genetic, familial aspect of heavy drinking in the parental home having its effect on the child, by way of example, is a much more potent factor' (Kessel and Walton 1989 p.64).

Behavioural Theories

If we turn towards other theoretical frameworks in order to understand heavy, dependent drinking, we may gain some different perspectives from psychological and behavioural theory. For instance, work has been done in animal experiments. Cats have been trained to move a switch to get food. In this experiment, on some occasions, a puff of air or an electric shock was given, instead of food, to induce emotional disturbance (Masserman and Yum 1946; Masserman, Yum *et al.* 1944). Those cats were then confronted with a choice between plain milk, or milk with alcohol. Under the influence of alcohol, they overcame their fear of moving the switch. The cats had learnt to take alcohol to relieve stress: their reward was a reduction, in human terms, of fear and anxiety. Similarly, it may be argued that the drinker takes alcohol to achieve certain rewards, both pharmacological (a feeling of euphoria and freedom from constraints) and social in that drinking draws people together and provides companionship and acceptance. Mello and Mendleson (1972) have demonstrated that many alcoholics do not maintain stable concentrations of blood alcohol when drinking, but rather (and indeed seek) considerable variation in blood alcohol levels. This suggests that the continuous change of state of being may be as desired and as rewarding as relief from physical or psychic difficulties, with the emphasis on feeling different.

The classic theory of Pavlovian conditioning might suggest that certain neutral stimuli can create both an association and a desire to drink. Meeting friends, time of day, particular places, smell of alcohol illustrate just a few of the many connections that trigger thoughts of drinking. Mello (1972) would support the idea that relapse to alcoholic drinking reflects conditioned behaviour rather than response to psychological conflict or just the desire to drink. It is possible to go further and show that the pharmacological effects of alcohol are conditioned. In an experimental setting, Marlatt, Demming and Reid (1973) showed that the amount of a vodka mixture consumed by a dependent drinker is determined by how much vodka that drinker thinks he is drinking rather than the actual amount of alcohol consumed. Further studies by Marlatt and Rohensow (1980) illustrated that the belief that one is drinking alcohol, even when one is not, may have much more bearing on the outcome of behaviour, for example aggression, relief of anxiety, sexual arousal, than the pharmalogical effect of alcohol *per se*.

Thus the fantasy or image around drinking can be created. Meeting friends triggers the desire to drink. Peer pressure and influence can reinforce that trigger and exaggerate the consequences, pushing an individual into a heavier drinking pattern than has been previously followed. Availability of alcohol in certain occupations – journalism, bar work, entertainment – may allow some people to drink at work and the work itself may then become a trigger to drink. So, too, thoughts about a stressful family, employment or financial situation may be sufficient stimulus to create the desire to drink alcohol.

Cultural Issues

Some would say that cultural factors are not strong enough in themselves to determine a drinking problem. However, they will have a bearing in a number of ways. Cultures that teach children responsible and ritualised drinking habits tend to have lower rates of alcohol abuse than cultures that forbid children to drink. Where drinking is accompanied by eating, and seen within a family context, as in France, the incidence of actual drunkenness is less high, and behavioural disturbances are less acute, although the risk of alcoholism with associated medical disorders remains very high. To refuse a drink in France is seen as unpatriotic, even ridiculous. France still experiences the highest rate of alcoholism in the world. The Italians, likewise, educate their children to diminish an alcohol 'high' by encouraging low proof alcohol, drinking with food and some parental restraint. However, the rate of alcoholism in Italy has steadily increased as the price of wine relative to income has steadily declined.

By contrast, other countries, notably Ireland, forbid children and adolescents from learning how to drink and yet go on to praise a heavy drinker in later years. As in Britain, the Irish prefer to drink in pubs, away from the family context, without and often before eating a meal, as individuals gather to meet fellow drinking partners. Therefore peer pressure increases with a residual need to express a sense of manliness by quantities consumed. Spirits and beer, consumed at speed, within a specific time 'before closing' contributes to the behavioural, drunken disorders that are all too commonly associated with drinking in Britain and North America. However, with the stringent drinking driving laws which now bear heavily on the societal aspects of drinking, and with extended opening hours which may reduce the speed at which some drink, acute drunkenness may possibly be less. Nonetheless, drinking too much is very hazardous.

So, it could be said that the 'cultural soil' has to be right for the seeds of an individual's alcohol abuse to develop. It is principally a problem in Western society where modern industrial society has contributed to destabilisation, cultural changes and family breakup. In the more religiously dominated cultures such as Moslem and Hindu, where alcohol is forbidden, the incidence of alcohol abuse is low.

Edwards (1974) points out that the use of any mood-altering drug results in behaviour that reflects a dynamic equilibrium between the culture and the drug's effects. He suggests that ritualized controlled social drinking will break down when any three of these conditions are met: when the culture itself is changing and loosening its control over individual members; when the sudden introduction of a substance with high dependence – inducing properties imposes a threat on an unprepared society; or when individuals, unresponsive to cultural influences use addictive drugs. His points are clearly demonstrated when examining the interface between Western cultures and those of other cultural strengths. For example, for the Native Americans and for the Eskimos and in many parts of Africa, there has been no physical, societal or psychological preparation for the impact of this highly influential drug and the consequences are clearly seen in high rates of alcohol abuse.

Availability and Price of Alcohol

Kessel and Walton (1989) clearly confirm that the more one individual drinks, the more alcohol abusers and alcoholics there will be in that society. If restrictions are imposed, through price, availability and/or societal attitudes and laws, the type and amount of drinking will change. It is interesting to reflect on the lessons learnt from the Prohibition in America. It seems this failed as the cultural norms would not tolerate such restrictions. Yet, in other cultures where it is the norm to prohibit alcohol, abuse is limited and perhaps confined to those who wish to rebel against those cultural restraints. That being said, it seems of interest that the same country that overturned the Prohibition was also the birthplace of Alcoholics Anonymous.

Price of alcohol, relative to income, will determine overall consumption. In Italy, as stated earlier, consumption has increased as relative cost has declined and in Britain, alcohol is cheaper, relatively, than at any time in history. Availability and accessibility of alcohol in Britain has increased enormously in the last decades, with longer drinking hours and a large range of alcohol on sale in shops and supermarkets.

Environmental Factors

Many would argue that greater availability of alcohol increases consumption but, again, other factors contributing to the desire to drink have to be considered in this equation. More of this is described in Chapter 3, but it is also important to consider the equation put forward by several authors (Vaillant 1983, Kessel and Walton 1989) which is:

Should the host be less resistant to the agent, there is greater risk of alcohol abuse. The environment, be it psychological, physical cultural or social has a major contribution to plain determining that resistance.

As has been suggested, cultural 'rules' of drinking may determine the type of problem encountered from alcohol excess. With high spirit, high speed consumption with no food will create greater potential for abuse as the central nervous system struggles to cope with the impact of the drug. Certain occupations which encourage or invite round-the-clock drinking – journalism, airline pilots, barmen – break down time-dependent drinking, exposing individuals to greater pressure to consume. Some occupations attract individuals who may wish to have an unsupervised life style: travelling salesmen, clubwork – perhaps to support an already established heavy drinking pattern.

Peer pressure, or pressure from the social group can powerfully affect an individual's drinking and therefore his or her potential for abuse. As with cultural factors, it has been shown that the potential for abuse comes as much from how and where the drinking takes place as from how much is actually imbibed. Those 'leading the pack' can be distinguished from his or her peers by social extroversion, dependence on peer-group pressure yet independence of parental or religious constraints (Jessor and Jessor 1975). Those leaders can put more vulnerable individuals at risk. However, the same can be said of movements and individual's who promote moderate drinking or abstinence. Alcoholics Anonymous is clearly illustrative of this.

Peer allegiance may influence behaviour. However, social isolation and social instability expose individuals to enormous risk. Cassel (1976) suggests that it is social demoralisation rather than poor social conditions or crowding *per se* that jeopardise social and family support. With the decline or absence of the latter, individuals are far more alone and more vulnerable to the solace of alcohol use and abuse. The increase of the young homeless in London in recent times bear witness to this tragic phenomenum.

Family Environment

As with cultural factors, the family environment create a miscrocosm with the same forces in play. Does parental drinking create the potential for abuse? Is alcohol abuse dependent on psychological forces present in the family settings? The authors of this book would strongly support the view that the development of the individual's attitude to alcohol is largely dictated by family attitudes and this is discussed at length in Chapter 3. However, Vaillant (1983), in his long and comprehensive study on the natural history of alcoholism would not see psychological and environmental forces as primary causative agents of alcohol abuse. He would argue that difficulties arise because of the distressing consequences of the problems created due to the dependency on alcohol. He does clearly illustrate, along with other authors, that there is an exact parallel between parental alcohol abuse and an individual's future risk of alcohol abuse. Out of 51 men who had few childhood environmental weaknesses – lack of love, instability, insecurity, violence – who did have an alcoholic parent, 27 per cent became alcohol dependent. Of the 56 men with many childhood environmental weaknesses, but who did not have an alcoholic parent, only five per cent became alcohol dependent.

When looking at the environmental factors that dictate or are seen to contribute to sociopathic behaviour – delinquency, criminal behaviour, difficulty in relationships, impulsivity, and those that are seen to contribute to incidence of alcohol abuse, if you take away the cultural forces and the alcoholic parenting, there is, according to Vaillant, little difference in the type of childhood experiences. Those with principally anti-social behaviour more commonly are found to have criminal fathers, and rejecting mothers. In alcohol abuse, close relationships with fathers are often rare and mothering inconsistent or over-dominating.

From these studies, issues are raised of whether it is the impact of the behaviour of the parent on the individual that determines future behaviour or whether it is the modeling of behaviour that is seen as acceptable, even laudable, by the youngster that leads to similar patterns. At a cultural level, there was a famous Catholic Priest in Ireland, Father Mathews, who promoted a vigorous campaign in favour of total abstinence. He achieved a remarkable following, until his death, when the movement almost totally disappeared. Contrary to this example, it was discovered that in the same study that looked at the incidence of alcohol abuse with an alcoholic parent, a significant number of those men with alcoholic ancestors were more likely to remain teetotal for their entire life time (Vaillant 1983) reminding us once more that many factors need to be considered together and that nothing is clear in isolation.

A change of economic circumstances may considerably affect an individual's attitude to life and, potentially, to drinking behaviour. An elderly person, adapting to retirement may find the economic and social adjustments very difficult, and resort to increased drinking despite financial constraints. For some, such constraints may limit drinking, although for others, the need for drink far extends their ability to fund the habit (see Chapter 8 dialogue 2).

Gender

Does gender make a difference to potential alcohol abuse? It has been well testified that men drink more than women (Dight 1976) although it seems that, in recent years, women have been able to declare their drinking more openly. Women do commonly drink at home, in secretive despair, attempting to hide their drinking from those returning home. This often suggests a daily pattern of slow drinking throughout the day resulting in a high consumption and maintaining levels of alcohol with little fluctuation. It is sometimes not detected or suspected for years.

Single men aged 45 and over are seen to be heavier drinkers than their married counterparts. This finding does not apply to women, where married and single middle aged women drink similar quantities (Kessel and Walton 1989). Alcohol metabolism is affected by gender difference. Women have a lower threshold to cirrhosis of the liver (Camberwell Council on Alcoholism 1980) and can endanger an unborn foetus if drinking continues through pregnancy. In most other respects, women will be prey to the same prevailing forces that will contribute to alcohol abuse – cultural, familial, psychological and emotional and many of the issues faced, in terms of the struggle it presents, will be equivalent to their male counterparts.

Adaptive Behaviour

Only under close scrutiny may the complex pattern of associations and influences become clear to the drinker and those around him. Indeed, such responses can become more akin to involuntary actions which remain repetitive and unchanging. Man, functioning at a high evolutionary level, has gained a capacity to respond imaginatively and with adaption to different situations and can glean from old experiences to make new ones. However, this inherent capacity is greatly compromised whenever drugs, trauma or psychological stress interfere with the possibility of adapting and responding (Blum 1966). The habitual drinker who is consistently blocking the ability to 'adapt' because of his use of alcohol will be trapped, unable to unlearn his addiction, and unable to learn a different response to stress. Does the drinker have a higher level of stress to handle? The cat experiment cited earlier in the chapter suggests that those who seek to drink to relieve discomfort are driven forward by forces and conflicts that are not altogether clear to the individual. The sources of such conflicts are explored in detail in Chapter 3.

The Helper within a 'System' – Implications for Intervention or 'Help'

We raise these factors that contribute to heavy drinking in order to address how best to approach the notion of 'help'. How can the helper best intervene in a complex system of causative and contributory factors? If dependent drinking is a 'disease', there will be a 'cure' and 'some medicine'. We might cite, as an analogy, the diabetic, who can regulate his insulin levels and lead a 'normal' life. We might attempt to apply the same model to the drinker who should, similarly, be able to regulate his alcohol intake and all would be fine. But, for almost anyone who misuses alcohol, and for anyone who is in contact with someone who abuses alcohol, this suggestion is entirely unrealistic.

For those who choose to stop drinking altogether, because their intake is out of control or because of other health, religious or cultural reasons, the pressure to 'join' the drinking world is continuous from both internal and external sources. This suggests that the causative factors in heavy drinking are dynamic and the need to find a way to explain the problem may vary from one individual to another. Intervention from the helper would necessarily vary according to their particular stance. If the disease model is adopted, 'I am an alcoholic, there is nothing I can do', intervention has to rely on acceptance of that fact, and clear advice about how to regulate alcohol intake must be given. This may be very successful or highly disastrous, depending on how the drinker 'takes the medicine'. The drinker can experience a considerable struggle to regulate or abstain. This again suggests that the situation is not static, and that what is perhaps needed is some help for that individual to find some of his own motivation to take responsibility for himself.

On the other side of the coin is the drinker who works hard at understanding and gaining insights in order that one day he will have so much control that he can regulate his own drinking. He is in danger of denying the physiological aspect of the 'disorder', and that danger can never be underestimated.

The Drinker within a 'System'

One way of seeing the causes of heavy drinking as dynamic is to examine the life context of the drinker. Although it may be seen that the drinker is carrying some stress, a contribution to that stress may lie within the 'system' in which he or she has been raised and/or is currently living. We refer here to the family. The family is a system which is comprised of many and complex parts, together making a whole. The family is a system in that a change in the behaviour and functioning of one member is automatically followed by compensatory change in another family member. This is true of all families, not just where drinking is taking place. 'Systems Theory' or 'Systems Thinking' (Von Bertalanffy 1968) when applied to families assumes that all significant people in the family unit play a part in the way family members function in relation to each other.

When the system is functioning healthily, emotional and behavioural adaptations absorb the new demands and needs of each individual in the family; parents adapt to their children's assertion of increased independence within the home; couples learn to adapt to the wife and mother taking on paid work; these and other changes mean that tasks around the house may need to be redistributed and routines adapted. The interaction and flexibility of roles can create a healthy creative environment which supports each member of the family system in asserting or maintaining individuality. So, a child starting school can go free of concerns for home, ready to make new relationships and engage in new experiences.

In a system where adaptations have to be made around some element of 'dysfunction', families may be able to compensate and adapt and may continue to function within the confines of that system (see Chapter 6, dialogue 1). For example, Dad loses his job through drinking, Mum finds work to help with family finances, Mum has less emotional energy for the child with school work, Dad gets the blame and all this then becomes family life.

Total dysfunction occurs when these adaptive processes break down and the flexibility in the system cannot cope with the strain. Mum gets exhausted supporting Dad and family. She loses her job, stays at home, becomes increasingly anxious, draws a protective response from the child, who then stays away from school. Hence all members of the family have their freedom curtailed, with consequential blame, resentment and fear.

It may be only at this point that the extent of the problems within the family is recognised, both by family members and those around them. Sometimes, it is 'the drinker' who is noticed. Sometimes it is the absenting child. Both are coping with the family anxieties in their own way. Perhaps, therefore, it is important to look at the whole system and not just the 'symptom carrier' in order to readdress the adaptations that have been made to help relieve the problems contributing to the drinking. The drinker may be carrying so much blame that he may not be able to adapt to a 'useful' role. Mum may have found some independence that she is reluctant to relinquish. The child may enjoy a 'special' relationship with Mum and be reluctant to let Dad back in on the scene. And then we ask Dad to stop drinking!

Undoubtedly, when 'others' become involved, be it the GP, the teacher, friend, counsellor, they too will become part of the system creating alliances, possible dependencies, jealousies. Intervention is necessary, and the impact of that intervention needs to be explored and thought through (see Chapter 5 and Chapter 6 dialogue 2) in order to realign the system in a way that can be beneficial to all. At times it is difficult to work out who has most invested in change. Often the person who 'should' be most concerned about solving the problem turns out to be least interested in doing so. Instead, another family member who is prepared to do something about finding a solution could be considered the 'client'. There can be a trap in family work of too easily finding a client and missing the distress of others.

The helper needs therefore to keep all aspects of the problem in perspective. The employment situation may need addressing; relationships within the family require exploring; or simply someone needs to be encouraged to walk down a different street away from the local bar. Within every individual lies the potential for change. That change will occur if the individual can respond to that which is around him. The helper needs to be clear what is the most appropriate response.

CHAPTER 3

'Am I Really that Different?'
Development of the Personality of the Drinker

Introduction

The development of an individual's personality is complex and determined by many factors – genetic predisposition, parental and environmental guidance, social and environmental circumstances. A tiny baby is born with strong and intense needs for whose fulfilment she is totally dependent on the outside world. And so the interaction between these factors and the individual begins. The scene is set for the journey from birth to maturity and independence. For some, the journey can be relatively straightforward. For others, it can be torrid and complicated.

For the drinker, something drives him to hide himself in alcohol in spite of clear indications that this is inappropriate and often foolhardy. His relationship with alcohol becomes more important than his relationship with others, however much he appears to be loved. Alcohol can promote a psychological dependency that has been likened to an infantile or regressed state. Certainly some of the humorous terms used to describe a state of intoxication commonly indicates this infantilisation – 'He was legless, paralytic', i.e., he could not walk. The alcohol addict has been described as 'never relinquishing the need for unconditional love' (Blane 1968). We shall examine some moments in the development of the individual where emotional difficulties may arise which will, in later years, lead to different sorts of manifestations of heavy drinking problems. While we recognise that there are different interpretations of this phenomenum which will undoubtedly dictate the approach adopted for its understanding, we see the ideas outlined in this chapter as fundamental to our thinking when addressing the concerns of drinkers.

The Early Years

A baby cries to communicate his distress. His needs are few, but intense and immediate. The response to those needs creates a relationship with the mother or 'carer' that lays down an associative, emotional and intensely experienced sense for that baby. Comfort, rage, frustration, despair, pleasure may be experienced according to how the infant perceives his demands being met. Each time a need is expressed, the infant's felt response will vary according to the source of the need and the emotional response from the carer. The integration of these emotional interactions will lay down the foundations of an individual's personality, which will, later in life, express and assert his own needs and interactions in relation to himself and others.

So, for the drinker, what's different? It has been well recognised that, for the drinker, parental care and guidance may have been in some way insufficient, misguided and inappropriate. In extreme cases, it has been overtly neglectful and cruel (Kessel and Walton 1989, Blane 1968), and so infantile needs are not fulfilled and rage, despair and anger are created.

When this expression is, in turn not comforted, the individual, for survival, adapts. His needs become buried, suppressed or even extinguished, and anxiety, emotional conflict and isolation are laid down as fundamental patterns in his personality (see Figure 3.1).

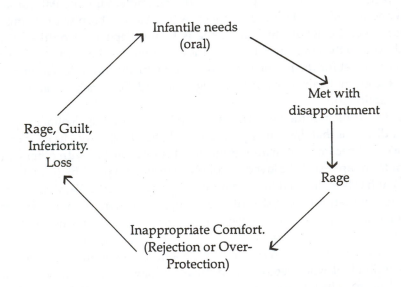

Figure 3.1.

There are many and intricate complexities to this phenomenon, depending on the type of interaction with the 'carer'. Comfort may be only temporarily withheld for a variety of reasons: premature birth, the infant's health, maternal illness or depression, maternal distraction by other siblings. Or, as shown by McCord and McCord (1960), caring may be consistently lacking and hostile due to maternal rejection and/or the mother's own drinking. The paternal figures of heavy drinkers have, in many cases, been harsh, punitive and emotionally absent, often, too, as a result of their own intoxication (Kessel and Walton 1989).

Emotional responses from a domineering mother and an ineffec[...] of behaviour from a paternal figure create a strong and dependent relatio[...] with the maternal figure, in which the infant constantly strives for love and affection. At the same time, the over-cautious, indulging carer smothers the infant's needs, denying the infant expression of feeling or assertiveness. It becomes a lifetime's struggle to establish any individuality and separation from a dominating albeit 'nurturing' maternal figure.

There is a consensus, however, that suggests that the most significant aspect in the development of the heavy drinker's problems is the inconsistency of care afforded by parental figures (Blane 1968). This may be, as suggested, due to parental drinking – one moment Dad is soppy and benign, the next he is full of rage. Mum may be frantic to 'keep things going' and becomes volatile and unpredictable under the strain. Or frequent and unexpected separations from important figures make the world unpredictable and uncertain, with different carers asking different expectations from the child.

If an appropriate response to the infant's needs is not made, at this very early stage, learning is adapted, frustration mounts, and progression into the next stage of development can be obstructed. In psychoanalytic terms, there is retardation of development at the oral stage, with conflicts and anxieties becoming deeply repressed. Furthermore, it has been suggested that failure at one stage of emotional growth impairs the development of the next stage as adaptations have to be made to compensate.

Distortions in the personality can result. The distortion will be the more severe the earlier the initial failure and the more numerous and far reaching the subsequent consequences (Blum 1966). A young person with poor parental guidance and poor emotional resources may find esteem with a group of drinking friends. It is at that point, with the discovery of alcohol in later life, that the unconscious connection to an unsatisfied oral need is revived and unconscious fulfilment (albeit pseudo-fulfilment) experienced.

In the principally dependent position, every infant's instinctual urges are focused on important figures in its world – mother, father. The instinctual wishes are invariably of opposing qualities with intense feelings of love and hate for the same person. This in itself is seen as a potent source of mental conflict as both the 'giver', i.e., the infant, and the 'receiver', i.e., the carer, have to tolerate the distress of the ambivalence.

For the future drinker, the 'hate' may be smothered by an overcautious carer – 'split off', i.e., buried or repressed. With the inconsistent and ambivalent carer, there is not sufficient comfort or support to begin to resolve the ambivalent feelings of the infant or the carer. The feelings of love and hate become chaotic and disconnected and both are buried as an attempt to create stability. In later life, it may be alcohol that becomes the constant and consistent 'object' of support that was denied by the carer, with the consequent release of chaotic and disconnected feelings of love and hatred, continuing the pattern of inconsistency in relation to those that are emotionally close.

Emerging Interaction with the World

Self protection and denial

From an early age, each individual's journey is different, and depending on the degree of extremes of emotional and cultural responses, further influences in development will be determined (see Chapter 2). Family circumstances may change, to allow the infant more consistent love and comfort. On the other hand, the inconsistencies in caring may remain the same and, as the child grows older, his response to the outside world will be defined by the need to defend himself from his inner turmoil and to cope with erratic caring, parental strife or physical punishment. The child's own needs may continue to be ignored, expression of those needs may be locked away, and a protection erected around them.

Commonly, for the future drinker, that protection is one of denial: 'I got home from school and there was no-one there: I didn't mind'. Behind that statement are the unspoken feelings of rejection, inferiority ('I can't be worth it') and low self-esteem. Expectations may become constantly eroded, with disappointments reoccurring that may add a feeling of hopelessness, despair and loss of trust. For the overprotected child, expression may become smothered in a different way, with the loss of spontaneous expression creating a slide into passivity and inactivity. 'Oh my mum will do that'.

In order to overcome feelings of rejection and inferiority, the individual may learn to overcompensate by developing a strong desire to please and gain approval. With this, an attempt is made to understand the surrounding confusion, and rationalisation creeps in: 'My dad hit me because he was drunk'. Perhaps as a response to fear of the confusion, a sense of bravado can develop: 'Do you want a fight?' At the same time, feelings of low self-worth can turn into guilt, and strong self-punitive ideas allow the anger (towards others) and shame for oneself to turn inwards: 'I can't do that, I will get into trouble'. Meanwhile, the protected child sails along untouched by the realities of the real world.

Confusion of self

With limited parental guidance for appropriate self expression, the child may find it less painful to avoid the intense need to explain himself. How often do we hear said: 'Oh do shut up and don't make a fuss'. It becomes unclear to the infant what it is acceptable to say or feel. So everything can become locked away, and the avoidance of emotional feelings becomes well established. However, these locked up feelings do not vanish. Unbeknown to the individual, they may become externalised, misplaced or 'projected' onto another person, in order to reduce the discomfort that those feelings create. At an unconscious level, the instinctual wishes and urges buried deep may be expressed in this way. Buried for so long, it feels far too dangerous to allow them to emerge into ordinary behaviour, yet they can emerge, especially when drinking. Unpredictable, extreme behaviour towards a loved one may be an example: (in an angry voice) 'You said you'd always love me', causes confusion, discomfort and hurt.

More overtly, there is a misplacement of harsh and punitive emotions that the individual has repeatedly received and needs to escape from. Blame, guilt, responsibilities, sadness can be readily assigned to others, thereby freeing the individual from his or her own distress: '*She* should have taken more care'; 'You look very unhappy today'. The identity of the individual can be totally submerged in this confused system, eroding any sense of self, and enhancing the void created in the early years (see Figure 3.2). Thus the evil can remain without, while the individual attempts to keep the good within. The boundaries between the perceived and the perceiver can become so blurred that there is no clarification between the two identities. Confusion can become absolute and hard to dislodge as it again creates an escape: 'My mum is always fantastic'.

With a decreased ability for spontaneous expression, the world seems cloudy and uncertain. Fear can be expressed by hostility 'I don't want to be your friend'. Rigidity creeps in to control emotional chaos. Trust is broken leading to suspicion, even paranoia, ('that chap is a liar') reducing the individual to an even greater isolation which he is now very ill equipped to handle.

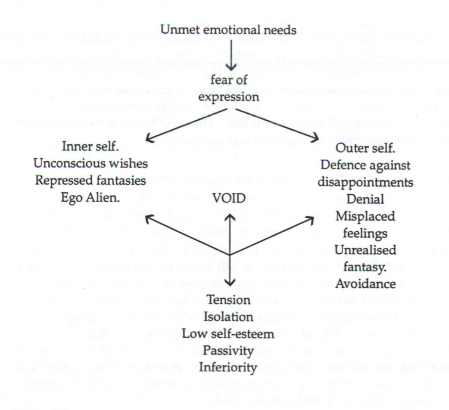

Figure 3.2.

Depending on the compilation of the factors of the individual's personality, a variety of different behaviours will manifest themselves: some people may become quiet, introverted, unambitious and 'stay at home with Mum'; some may display overtly unusual behaviour, for example bed wetting, or intense agitation as a way of handling distressing or unpleasant memories. Others may slide into relationships that will seemingly take care of them in a way that has not been experienced before. But in all these cases, the 'self' is lost.

Outside Influences

Undoubtedly, important factors other than internal issues abound through the developmental journey. Parental behaviour or 'models' will influence the small child, and the expression of that behaviour will occur through, for example, their sexual and marital relationships, their attitudes to work and to politics and, of course, their attitude to alcohol. Hore (1976) suggests that imitation of behaviour surrounding individuals can contribute significantly. Heavy drinking contributes to inconsistency, unpredictability and extremes of emotional expression. Violence, self preoccupation, rage, guilt and deceit can become exacerbated. So, some individuals, experiencing such a situation, may have to deal with the inconsistencies of their emotional world. At the same time, they may also learn to imitate extreme forms of behaviour. There will be variations of degree in expression of parental behaviour, but it must be argued that the impact of the behaviour will influence the development of the individual experiencing the consequences. Parental behaviour will be dictated by their own experiences as children and by their own defences erected against the world: 'Oh blow this, I am off to the pub'. The child from the next generation will be interacting with this and will learn and respond.

Expression of Emotional Conflict through Alcohol

The discovery of alcohol in later life – at any period in life – can appear to fill a void that is deeply felt but has, hitherto, been hidden behind strong defences. The timing and the occasions for the connection between the drug alcohol and relief from psychic pain are infinitely variable. They will differ for every individual. For some, the connection will never be made. But, as suggested earlier, it is those exposed to the heavy drinking of a parent or 'carer', and to the emotional consequences of such behaviour, and those whose own development was disturbed at the earliest stages and who have access to alcohol who will make the psychological connection with the 'comforts' of drinking earliest. They have a need to deny an unpleasant reality and a need to turn it into something pleasurable. Through lack of love, they tend to be self-centred, absorbed by self-love (or narcissistic), impulsively searching for a primary focus of loving comfort. They find this in alcohol.

Some drinkers may appear obstinate, aggressive, rebellious by nature, reminiscent of characteristics of children who are struggling to gain independence through walking, talking, and achieving sphincter control. If there is mismanagement of emotional needs at this stage of the child's development, the conflict and anxiety experienced may become repressed or diverted away from expression. Alcohol may, in later life, release infantile feelings that have never been expressed, and the resulting behaviour may well be incompatible with the chronological age of the drinker (Blum 1966).

The child who is learning to walk and talk is becoming more socially adaptive, less 'self-centred', and beginning to interact more freely with others of both sexes: men, women, boys, girls. If, at this time, the expression of the interaction is incompatible with parental expectations and desires, anxieties and conflicts may be generated (for example, big boys don't cry). The expression of love and intimate feelings, especially towards members of the same sex, may become associated with conflict and anxiety and become diverted away from complete expression; it may reappear, in later life, in a maintenance of same sex friendships. Or, a repression of homosexuality may occur (Blum 1966). Alcohol may, however, break through the diversion (or sublimation) and an expression of homosexual tendencies in an undisguised form may be observed in intoxication. Irrational fears of same sex friendships and unjustified hatred for homosexuals may point to strong repressive manoeuvres to keep an unconscious attraction at bay. And for some, drinking may be used as a defence against the discomfort of these feelings and as a confirmation of sexuality.

For men, problems may emerge that arise from unresolved conflicts towards their mothers. In adulthood, their relationships may be impaired by the unresolved feelings of tenderness and sexuality which they cannot direct toward the same woman, the origins of which would have been feelings towards their own mothers. They assume many superficial relationships, are overtly affable and helpful, but barely hide repressed anger, fear of sexual inadequacy, low self esteem and competitiveness. Such men experience difficulties with authority figures, rekindled by the unresolved feelings of jealousy and impotence that they felt towards their fathers. They turn to alcohol to alleviate these discomforts, which, in its turn, only deepens the problems of forming meaningful relationships.

Some personality structures can become entrenched, drawing alcohol into that structure (see Figure 3.3). The 'Self Indulgent' that have been pampered and protected, drink to release the hate that has never been expressed, to overcome frustrations, to avoid any expression of conflict and to rediscover, in adult life, the all embracing maternal care, which takes them into a fantasy world and allows them to escape the realities of obsolete relationships (Kessel and Walton 1989). The person with sexual problems may take alcohol either in the hope that it will help him or her to achieve a 'normal' satisfactory sexual encounter, or will drink to relieve the guilt and shame if that has not happened.

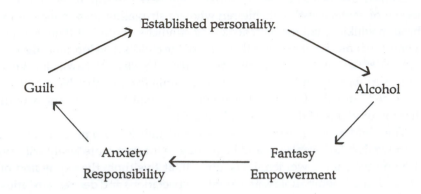

Figure 3.3.

Those whose angry and hostile feelings have been suppressed by parental control find expression very difficult. When they are keen to protest because of provocation or humiliation, a sense of impending punishment causes such tension that they resort to drink for escape. When intoxicated they are commonly aggressive, releasing the hostile impulses that are normally kept so tightly in check. When sober, there is total astonishment at such behaviour. As suggested earlier, excessive dependence on parental figures prevents successful maturation. Those who do not break away, in spite of success at school, do not achieve. Some remain self-centred, others need constant approval and alcohol may offer some relief from the sense of being eternally trapped.

It is well recognised that we commonly re-enact, with a partner, the relationship that is reminiscent of that of our parental model. Although consciously we often strive not to replicate former models, unconscious manoeuvres may unwittingly force us into that repetition. If the needs in the primary relationship have not been fulfilled, there is unconscious longing to find solace. However, in the re-enactment, the same mistakes are often made. Hence the cycle may be repeated and the primitive rage and resentments be rekindled. Alcohol may facilitate an expression of that rage and indeed become a source of comfort otherwise unobtainable.

Why Alcohol?

As described in Chapter 1, alcohol is absorbed directly into the bloodstream. Its effects are almost immediate. It is often said amongst drinkers: 'that pint didn't have time to touch the sides of the glass' – an evocative image of the immediacy of need and gratification. It is the combination of the speed of its absorption and its releasing properties – because of its depressant effect (see Chapter 1) – that makes alcohol so attractive. Just as the bulimic, or overeater, feels 'stuffed' and comforted by food, so the drinker feels 'filled' and untrapped. But it is the very same properties of speed of absorption and release that makes alcohol potentially so dangerous. How often have we heard friends say, after a few drinks, 'Oh, I'm OK to drive'. It is not that they are lying; they have genuinely lost the capacity to make an informed and reasonable judgment, because they have had a drink. Denial has already set in. The understanding of behaviour and personal interaction is lost until the next morning, when some clarity dawns, with possible guilt, anxieties and recriminations pressing hard – the very reasons why alcohol was sought in the first place.

Alcohol becomes important *because* it releases people from conflict created by defences erected during their development. But because of the resulting drinking, those defences will be exacerbated and become yet more entrenched. The individual is searching for escape. Alcohol provides a brief reprieve, but, at the same time, cold reality becomes harsher and more escape is sought. Pent up feelings of rage and resentment can, under the influence of alcohol, get released and misdirected, leading to violence, crime and all the known social disasters of brutality to men, women and children. If this is not harmful enough, the individual loses the capacity to express him/herself without the presence of alcohol: 'I can't stand this, I'm off to the pub!'

Alcohol takes on a life of its own as the individual retains less and less capacity and awareness to handle its consequences. 'It's the drink that is making me talk/bad/act this way'. It becomes an object of desire and hate simultaneously: 'I could murder a drink'. Alcohol becomes a target for misplaced feelings of responsibility and blame, formerly laid at others' feet: 'If it wasn't for the drink, I could get a job/be happy, etc'. This enables the drinking to continue. The misplacement can become so strong that the individual is once again trapped: 'I never want to try that again. I will never trust another person'. Rigidity, inflexibility and an entrenched lifestyle dependent on alcohol become the norm. There is great reluctance to be different, because the unconscious needs, far from being resolved, are buried even deeper, although guilt and remorse can speak otherwise: 'I am sorry, I do promise to stop'. Drinking itself is a resistance to change as it prevents the possibility of personal exploration and therefore recovery. Stopping drinking is seen by the 'ego' or self as a new danger, because of the threatening issues that have to be faced (Sandler, Dare and Holder 1973). So alcohol continues to confuse an already fragile, vulnerable personality structure.

Forming Relationships

Before, during and after the emergence of drinking behaviour, relationships may be formed in a quest for support and satisfaction. It is fair to say that most relationships in life are entered into with little clarification of the true needs of the two parties involved. This is true, too, for the drinker. As a relationship progresses, a clearer picture will emerge. For the individual 'tied to the apron strings', a normal transition into an intense relationship may prove impossible.

Others may dive quickly and impulsively into a relationship that seems embracing and caring.

With the realisation (albeit unconscious) that suppressed frustrations and neediness cannot be met within the partnership, rage and disappointment from former days may return. The uncertainty or ambivalence of the love and hate experienced within the relationship with the primary figure may be re-enacted, the 'hate' being too dangerous to express in sobriety yet too intense to ignore. Drinking may start to force a wedge between the now precarious bond, which may now have to deal with the erratic, unpredictable and disinhibited behaviour of the drinking partner. This may come as a total surprise to both parties: 'She was so placid when I met her'.

At the point within a relationship that is reminiscent of difficult and unresolved points in maturation, one of the parties may seek solace in alcohol, though this will depend to some extent on the level of maturity of both parties. The birth of the first child, or subsequent children, may arouse acute envies; the death of a parent, retirement, redundancy may trigger feelings that have been, hitherto, 'held' in the relationship, but that only alcohol can now assuage. This may be in secret, and kept that way for many years, as disclosure of self becomes increasingly difficult.

For the established drinker, it is often said: 'I was drunk when I met her' or 'She knew I was a drinker when I married her' – in other words, there is some knowledge of this behaviour, even some attraction to it. How can this be so? It can be said in humour: 'Oh you have married your mother/your father'. In drinking families this is very explicit. A woman with a heavy drinking father will have this as a model of behaviour. As a result, she may have been emotionally deprived, even physically abused. Her needs, in a relationship, may then be twofold: a need to 'rescue' a man with whom she is infatuated from the alcoholic hell her own father experienced; and, as the expression of her own needs has become so confined, she can only recognise them and indeed see their expression in another.

Likewise, the drinker is looking for someone who will retain control and take responsibility in order to perpetuate his own drinking. So their emotional needs are mutually compatible, each providing a harbour for the boat the other cannot row themselves. Commonly, in a marriage of this nature, one partner is a heavy drinker and the other is teetotal. 'I will drink while you keep control'. 'I will look after you if you express my frustrations'.

The above is a vivid example of what is termed a mutually held projective system. This forms the basis of every relationship and will be expressed in a multitude of ways depending on the combination of the needs of the two parties, with many and subtle complexities and influences (see Chapter 6, dialogue 1 and Chapter 9, dialogue 1). So much can be learnt and understood by the exploration of a relationship. Likewise, it is important to see an individual in the context of all his relationships, even with alcohol, for any real assessment to take place. Once drinking has started, within a relationship, there will be the hurts, the guilt, the worries. Both inside and outside of that relationship, the drinker, while drinking, remains alone.

CHAPTER 4

'How Can I Help?'
The Relationship Between the Drinker and the Helper

Each word of the title of this chapter 'How can I help?' can readily carry emphasis for exploration of different aspects of this important question. '*How* can I help' lays emphasis on what resources and expertise are available and on the practical ways forward. 'How *can* I help' suggests some sense of the magnitude of the difficulties that drinking problems pose and questions whether I *shall* be allowed to help. With emphasis on the 'I', an assessment of the qualities, commitment and confidence of the helper or carer is thrown into relief, raising responses ranging from humility and uncertainty to positive strength and determination. And with emphasis on the final word of this question, another range of issues is suggested for there is, sadly, a societal stereotyped response that *help* for the drinker can be a waste of time. The declaration of a professional involvement in working with drinkers often evokes some such response as: 'Is it not depressing?' or 'What is the success rate like?' with a hidden suggestion that failure is high. How often is this question asked of other groups of people in need?

The implication seems to be that drinking problems are self-inflicted whilst other major health problems resulting from a choice of life style are intrinsically different. For example, although it is too late to tell the gentleman in cardiac failure that he has been on an unhelpful diet for many years, all the cardiac facilities are put immediately at his disposal because it is a 'medical' emergency and in a medical emergency, everyone is usually treated alike. However, in the case where an alcohol problem is discovered to be an underlying feature, or that person has merely had too much to drink, attitudes may be very different. The task of this chapter is to look at different aspects of how 'help' can be provided and to define what is not of help, for all too often an alcohol problem is ignored or put aside.

Finding Resources

Before starting to 'talk', it is helpful to have an idea of the sorts of information and resources that are available to 'help' the drinker. Some facts about consumption and the risks posed by heavy drinking may be all that is needed (see Chapter 1). There are leaflets, books and videos available for information (a list is provided at the back of this book). Contact numbers for telephone advice can be found in the telephone book, or at the local doctor's surgery, Citizens Advice Bureau or Samaritans. Local counselling, voluntary and statutory agencies will vary from area to area. It may be a good investment to discover what is available and have at hand information to give out. In our experience, members of Alcoholics Anonymous (AA) and Al-Anon are always happy and willing to discuss and talk. They have a fund of knowledge based on personal experience. They know what has helped them and are willing to share this knowledge to help others. They are willing to introduce people to the fellowship and are only too aware of the difficulties experienced by an individual who is taking the first steps towards help.

How Can I Help? – The Problems of Raising Questions

The drinker, in simple terms, has problems in his relationship with alcohol. At the same time, the relationship between the drinker and the drug is exclusive, well known and 'reliable' and, to that extent, it is satisfactory to the drinker. The helper may be seen as disturbing stability if the drinking is addressed and, having asked the drinker to question his drinking, he may well be required to 'take the place of' the drink as a source of ever-present support. Both these possibilities can seem daunting. Furthermore, questioning someone's drinking is more far-reaching than suggesting to a friend that eating too much fat may cause heart problems. For both the drinker and the helper, fear of exposure is central. The drinker, if drinking is acknowledged, has to begin to contemplate change and then drinking will itself become a token of resistance to that change. For the helper, the issues are also manifold. First, to question someone's drinking can be embarrassing; after all, it is a socially acceptable habit, a token of generosity and camaraderie. Also, in questioning another's drinking, the helper may then have to consider his own drinking habits. At a deep, even unconscious level, personal issues of dependency may have to be wrestled with. It can be a defence against the helper's own emotional issues that the drinking in another is not challenged.

The drinker (as with most in need) and the drinker's behaviour prompts us to see aspects of ourselves. Two reflections have already been highlighted thus far – fear and denial – and the extent to which the helper acknowledges these and other reflections can be crucial in influencing *how* the *help* is given.

Every relationship, through interaction, will consist of emotional, intellectual, and spiritual expression concurrent with both individuals' defences to that expression. As illustrated in Chapter 3, someone who is teetotal may develop a significant relationship with a heavy drinking partner for reasons dictated by her own needs and history – for example, to 'rescue' her partner from the hell her own father went through, and/or for the drinker to express for her what it feels too risky to say for herself. This is called 'projective identification'.

Without considerable self-exploration and self-understanding, no helper or carer can be outside of, or not party to this powerful form of interaction. Self-exploration leads to an emerging recognition that the helper or carer goes into a specific type of work by choice, albeit a choice to fulfil unconscious needs, in much the same way as the teetotal wife has chosen her heavy-drinking partner. Unconsciously, the helper is saying to his drinking client: 'I will look after you, if you look after the part of me that I cannot look after myself'. The drinker does that for himself by drinking. The helper may be achieving this by looking after the drinker.

This identification can promote tremendous empathy and understanding of the drinker's plight – a vital ingredient for 'help'. Hence the success of important self-help groups such as Alcoholics Anonymous. Empathy can prompt intervention, which can undoubtedly help an individual on to the road to recovery. Patience, tolerance and compassion can lead to hours of listening; the empathetic, rather than the sympathetic, the conditional rather than the unconditional helper is more likely to achieve. Unconditional sympathy may indicate that the helper is too identified with the drinker to recognise that the drinker needs to take responsibility to enable change to come about.

It is at the point when the interaction begins to shake the foundations of the helper's strengths that difficulties may emerge. Sadly, what can happen is that the drinker gets blamed for the 'problems' – 'Oh he is so demanding': 'She is wasting my time'. Indeed, drinkers can be demanding: that is the nature of their distress. But such comments may tell us more about the difficulties the helper may be having in responding to those demands, rather than offering us a clear assessment of the drinker's personality. Because those difficulties may be unrecognised, the helper may be more prone to emphasise the reluctance to change in the other, to project his own feelings onto the drinker and so reinforce the vicious circle. It is therefore important for all those involved with drinkers to search for some self-understanding through friends, colleagues, informal supervision and self-help groups such as Al-Anon. This topic is discussed further in Chapter 5.

Another aspect of drinking which inhibits effective intervention is the disinhibited, forthright nature of intoxication. 'In vino veritas', it may be said, but the sight of a drinker on a park bench, homeless and dirty, is a stark reminder of the vulnerability of mankind. Reactions vary. 'It is disgraceful'.

'They should be locked away'. 'There but for the Grace of God go I'. Some people are angry, some apologetic, but both those reactions defend against that part of self that is seen in that human suffering. Even very heavy drinkers will say: 'Well, I can't have a problem; I'm not on a park bench'.

Because of the challenging nature of the drinkers expression, the helpers response tends to be acute: 'I can't cope with drinkers': 'Look at the dreadful conditions these people have to live in'. It is because of the numerous mirrors that drinkers provide and the apparent and real neediness of their plight, that the helper may not help them move towards changing for fear of releasing a burden of intense dependency needs – the very thing the helper may be fearful of. If the helper is seduced, through personal identification, into not challenging the drinker's behaviour, she loses some therapeutic objectivity.

In this case, the bond of the relationship remains with alcohol rather than with the helper, who is reduced to colluding with the drinker. Clearly, in some situations, the helper has no other option than to 'manage' the intoxicated – a wife with a drunk husband, a nurse in a casualty department (see Chapter 6 dialogue 2 and Chapter 9 dialogue 2) – but even in these difficult situations, the helper can only be effective by communicating concern for the individual's plight while not being pushed, through persuasive or even violent means into condoning drinking behaviour. The drinker may plead, 'But I didn't touch the whisky' meaning, 'that's my usual tipple and therefore I have been good'. If collusion takes place, the relationship with alcohol remains unchecked. No answer may be better than giving the wrong impression.

Even in an apparently positive situation where the drinker clearly states a desire to change and is engaged in regular counselling, secret drinking may be happening. A helper's resistance, to challenge this, may be expressed as: 'Oh but she is doing so well. Questioning her may damage our relationship'. But if the helper does not ask about drinking, the drinker may not volunteer the information. The drinker does not want to let the helper down and the helper fears the drinker's hostility in raising the subject, when progress is apparently being made. The drinker can sometimes hide behind the issue of trust. 'You don't trust me, do you?' However, it is the drinking that is damaging the relationship, not the helper. As a resistance to and fear of change, the drinker will unconsciously seek this position. The helper needs regular personal assessment to clarify whose is the resistance and whose is the fear (see Chapter 5).

Clarifying the Process of Interaction

It is sometimes tempting to provide for the drinker by making allowances for him: to protect, to find accommodation, make appointments, even buy him 'just the last one'. Without disputing the generosity and care that is thankfully extended to drinkers in different spheres, it throws into relief a phenomenon that is attributable to all relationships and of particular importance when exploring talking to drinkers.

On meeting, there can be a noticeable tendency for one party to relate to the other AS IF they were talking to someone else. In psychodynamic terms, this process is called *transference*. The 'as if' quality is usually connected to experiences of past relationships, commonly ones of significant power, such as with parents or teachers. This can be expressed simply and clearly: 'You remind me of a teacher I once had', or with much greater complexity: 'What do you want of me?' meaning, 'I do not know what is expected of me. Things have never been made clear to me and I feel scared and confused'. Or, when asked about himself, the drinker feels inhibited and tongue-tied: 'I feel too frightened to express myself'. Depending on the quality and type of experiences the drinker has had with 'significant others', his behaviour will be determined and high-lighted in all interactions with the helper.

If intoxicated, these 'transferences' may be emphasised through aggression, seductiveness, helplessness. In sobriety, they will remain, albeit expressed less overtly, indicating the difficulties that the drinker may have with personal relationships and expression of feelings. Hostility, defiance, resentment, charm, persuasiveness, suspicion may come across to the helper. Not only does the pattern of these feelings and reactions suggest how a drinker hides his difficul-ties, but may also suggest how that individual has been with others most of his life – a valuable aspect to understand, if a clearer picture of where difficulties may have originated is to be acquired.

The helper will naturally have a response. The strength of the 'as if' quality in the drinker's interaction creates a varied and extreme response in those with whom he has contact. Suspicion, resentment, even professional dread or warmth, sensitivity and empathy can be polarised within an individual helper or within a staff team. Likewise, the helper will be responding to some of his personal and professional vulnerabilities in relation to the demands of the drinker, as well as their own 'as if' experiences that are raised by the presence of the drinker as a person. All relationships are a roundabout of confused interactions and there is further explorations of these interactions in the dia-logue chapters of this book (Chapters 6–11). To help the helpers, clarification of their responses is vital and this is discussed in Chapter 5. To help the drinker, clarification of what he is saying and feeling will be important too.

The drinker may come to the helper fearful of authority, guilty about his drinking, feeling low and saying, 'I have slipped again, I am wasting your time'. The helper may recognise the drinker's low mood (perceptive) and say, 'You seem very low' reflecting a perceived feeling; or she may be inwardly irritated that the drinker has let her down again (on reflection she realises that her father was constantly letting her down) and say 'You are not wasting my time'. Maybe here the helper is experiencing some angry denial. Alternatively, the helper may say, 'Don't feel guilty, you've come to the right place'. Here there may be some unrecognised identification with the feeling of guilt.

There is never a right or a wrong way to react, although some responses will be more helpful than others. If the helper is really listening only to the drinker, he will hear that the drinker feels low, he feels guilty, he feels that he is a waste of time and there is an expectation of some kind of retribution for failing. It may be helpful for the helper to tell the drinker what he hears: 'It sounds to me as if you feel guilty, fed up with yourself and that I might be cross with you for letting me down'. Having clarified some feelings, it may then be possible to establish some action: 'It may be important to come to the Day Centre/ go to AA/ come and see me next week to help you get back on your feet'.

As the helper may remind the drinker of past experiences, he may be held in some 'awe' or authority, as were parents or teachers in the past. Inwardly, the drinker may feel powerless and thereby empower the helper through his own sense of weakness and through an inappropriate transference of his fears of authority. Some drinkers hide this powerlessness by presenting with belligerence and hostility towards institutional authority such as the police or casualty departments, transferring onto them their experience of authority from the past.

It is not only the police that can be challenged in this manner. The drinker feels empowered by drinking. In the face of the intoxicated, the helper can feel disempowered. In sobriety, the tables can turn. The use and/or abuse of power may rest wholly with the helper. Have we turned someone away when seeking help 'to pay him back' for drinking? Do we use our seniority to persuade the team that Mrs X needs help at all costs? (see Chapter 9 dialogue 2 and Chapter 8 dialogue 2). Firm limits need to be clarified for drinkers and helpers alike in order not to continue to disempower individuals that seek help and thereby perpetuate the drinking.

Setting Limits

In drink, life becomes confusing, chaotic and bewildering. Habitual drinkers become used to this life style and considerable energy goes into counteracting the consequences: 'I'm sorry I'm late, I just...' For some, unpredictability in childhood was the norm. For others, rigorous attention smothered all sense of adventure. Because the drinker seeking help comes with his own chaotic difficulties and with past experiences that may dictate his response to the helper, the issue of consistency and boundary-keeping is of great importance.

Alcohol, when misused, crashes through every social barrier that exists, by violence, drunken driving, deceit, and may destroy any offers of help if it is allowed. The drinker may anticipate chaos from others because that is what he is used to. Indeed, he may provoke it to feel more secure and to prevent a realisation of his own chaos. He may, for instance, turn up at the GP's surgery, knowing that Dr X is on holiday and insisting on seeing Dr Y who does not know him so well. Alternatively, the drinker may have very high expectations of a worker to 'never let him down' finding anything other intolerable to bear.

Setting limits on others can at times feel unreasonable, even punitive. It is often only in hindsight that limits can be deemed helpful or unhelpful. For example, a man presents for admission at an alcohol treatment unit. Here it is the rule that once on the premises, all those admitted are asked not to leave the building. This helps to define ambivalence towards treatment and facilitates the observation of withdrawal symptoms. The said man, however, argues persistently for some forty-five minutes for permission to go to the bank. This seems, on the surface, a reasonable request: he wants money for tobacco. A week later, he is able to acknowledge that he was searching, albeit unconsciously, for an excuse to go and drink. The clear limits imposed enabled him to confront his uncertainty about facing change.

Creating limits promotes safety. Speed limits are imposed for social safety; the price of goods are clearly marked so that the shopper knows where he stands and can make a clear choice about his purchase. Life without limits contributes to confusion and possible harm, uncertainty and loss of trust. Personal safety, on the other hand, creates a sense of peace. In a therapeutic setting, the establishment of a state of trust is seen as a basic requirement, especially for those who have experienced repeated deprivation (Erikson 1950). The framework for that trust has to be created by the helper in order, first, not to repeat past patterns for the drinker and second, to enable the formation of some form of treatment alliance.

When a helper meets someone who is inebriated, that person is likely to have lost some control. By clarifying what is acceptable, i.e., what the helper will tolerate and what the helper can offer, the helper can provide the foundation for trust that the drinker may crave but cannot find in herself or in others. A nurse in a GP's surgery may helpfully say: 'I can bandage your leg, but I cannot help you with your stomach pain here. I think you need help to stop drinking'. Sandler, Dare and Holder (1973) suggest that 'the ability to develop a treatment alliance is thought to draw on qualities which have become a relatively stable part of the individual'. In a personal relationship, the same issues apply. Clarification of what a partner or friend can or cannot tolerate is vital to prevent the 'drinking' from destroying the relationship irrevocably.

There may be understandable fear on the part of the helper that events may get out of hand and the temptation may be to back off from the difficult task of setting limits. As a result, the nature of the fears for both drinker and helper are never addressed or explored. However, no-one can be expected to define limits all the time without support. Having basic understanding can add to personal confidence in handling tricky situations, and working towards such understanding with friends, colleagues and superiors provides 'help' (see Chapter 5).

The Process of Assessment

Having explored some of the different theoretical issues that may help us understand the relationship between the drinker and the helper, we turn now to tabulating and listing some aspects of assessment which may help us glean more insight into the drinker's plight. Good and clear understanding of circumstances helped by careful assessment can assist effective management of any given situation. Yet the word 'assessment' can inspire feelings of apprehension, a sense of judgment for both drinker and helper from past experiences of school, job interviews, or even from visiting 'the carers'. A sense of failure can be in the air.

- For the helper – 'What if I get it wrong?' 'What if I don't get all the facts?'
- For the drinker – 'What have I done wrong?'

It is important to remember that assessment is a continuous process for both parties. It will take time and possibly several meetings for information to be gathered and exchanged.

Although a sensitive assessor will bear these aspects in mind, this is by no means the whole picture. In a well-conducted interview, enormous progress can be made by the drinker towards a clarification of his problems. An assessment must meet the needs of both the helper and the drinker (Edwards 1982). It therefore needs to include:

1. The establishment of a relationship between helper and drinker

All assessments will draw on the disclosure of personal information. For the drinker, this may be the first time or opportunity to admit to himself, let alone anybody else, that he has a problem related to drink. The fear of attack, humiliation, embarrassment may be huge. The strength of the defences against the anxiety of the situation may be greater than usual and so the helper needs to 'invite the surrender of defences' (Edwards 1982).

With sensitivity to the relationship, the helper can gain important clues as to how the drinker approaches others. The helper may ask himself what this relationship feels like. Is it friendly, fearful, slow, chaotic? 'How does the drinker react to me and how do I make him feel?' From this, some understanding of the drinker's life's journey and his relationship with alcohol can be gleaned. His ability to understand his own journey and to make connections with important events in his life, and the situation in which he finds himself can be explored and discussed. At times this can create great relief. However, if the drinker is intoxicated, the process of assessment is distorted. And it is therefore always advisable, if possible, to see the individual again when sober. He will gain far more. If he is intoxicated, he will remember very little and he is the one that is searching for help.

2. The opportunity to gain a clear picture and understanding of the present situation

Openness from the helper will allow the drinker greater freedom to declare himself and discuss his position openly. Clearly, different situations will demand the need for different information depending on where, why and how the assessment takes place: there may be a need for assessment for admission into hospital, or it may be someone presenting for residential accommodation but, whatever the case, it is an opportunity for the drinker to gain information, ask questions, ask advice, gain insight and come to some self assessment or appraisal which he can grasp and make use of. The drinker may have been through many assessments in his life or this may be the first but, whatever the circumstances, it is important for both parties to seize the moment for exchange of ideas and information. It is also important to understand the individual as an individual in his own right, in the context of his present (family, job, lifestyle), in the context of his past and in the context of his drinking.

Below is a list of examples of some of the issues both drinker and helper may need to discuss. The issues are not set out in order of priority and are included to alert the helper to the existence and extent of an alcohol problem. Exclusion or avoidance of topics (by either the drinker or the talker) need to be considered as relevant to the assessment.

Request for help with drink problem – has that come from individual, family member, other professional?

Current understanding of the problem by the individual – attitude to a drinking problem.

Presentation – smell of alcohol, restlessness, distractibility.

Physical health – e.g. fit, wheezy, overweight/underweight.

Symptoms of addiction – 'shakes', the need for a drink, blackouts (see Chapter 1).

Duration of existing problems – brief drinking history.

Current drinking pattern – quantities, times, type of drink, solitary, social, change of pattern.

Physical disorders – e.g. ulcers, peripheral neuropathy (see Chapter 1).

Family situation – married,single, divorced, living with parents, living within another's family. Nature of the relationships with significant partners.

Children – nature of the relationships. Neglect, truancy, emotional disturbance.

Accommodation – family home, rented, hostel, homeless.

Personal History – significant life events. problem drinking in family, including grandparents and children.

Childhood – a flavour of the individual's experience.

Education – experience and qualifications.

Employment – history, type and current situation.

Problems at work – e.g. unemployment, absenteeism, overworking.

Emotional difficulties – anxiety, depression, suicide attempts, hospitalisation.

Past help received – in childhood, for other addictions (e.g. drugs) problems with physical illness, psychiatric help, self/family.

Criminal record – e.g. drunken driving, petty theft, domestic strife.

Accidents – in the home, at work, road traffic accidents.

USE OF OTHER DRUGS

A vital issue to be considered in an assessment is the use of other drugs. The drinker may be turning to other drugs to help him maintain his sobriety or they may be taken as a substitute for alcohol, to minimise his drinking, or to enhance the effects of alcohol. While there are many drinkers who are prescribed medication for legitimate reasons, there are some who may persistently request sleeping tablets or tranquilisers. Once the acute phase of the withdrawal syndrome has passed, for which 'replacement medication' is very necessary to prevent fitting and some of the very unpleasant experiences of withdrawal, further prescription is, in the long term, unhelpful.

The drinker will learn to depend on an alternative to alcohol, will not have the opportunity to experience a drug-free existence and may develop another addiction. It can be easy for the helper to collude with this with the best intentions. It 'seems' to help the drinker to be less panicky and get a good night's sleep, but this action also prolongs psychological dependency and delays the moment for the addiction to be confronted. All use of drugs must be discussed on assessment.

3. Empathy

The helper needs to work hard at imagining what it is like to be 'Mr Morris', who has recently lost his wife after 35 years of marriage, or 'Mrs Jones' who lived in a small house on a busy road with her grandparents because her father was always drunk, or those individuals featured in the dialogue chapters of this book. Stepping into others' shoes can speak louder than any words.

Clues from the following list may help another to understand what it is like to BE Mr Morris or Mrs Jones (see Chapter 7 dialogue 2) and what is therefore the nature of their struggle:

- Eye contact
- Gait
- Dress
- Smell
- Posture
- Concentration
- Physique – weight, complexion
- Restlessness/anxiety
- Type of speech – speed, content.

4. Assessment of dependence on alcohol

(a) PSYCHOLOGICAL DEPENDENCE (SEE CHAPTER 8 DIALOGUE 1)

The CAGE four item screening test enables the helper to cover the important aspects of psychological dependence (Macleod, Mayfield and Hay 1972).

C. – **Cutdown** – Have you ever needed to *cutdown* on your drinking?

A. – **Annoyed** – Have you ever felt *annoyed* about others criticising your drinking?

G. – **Guilty** – Have you ever felt *guilty* about your drinking?

E. – **Eyeopener** – Have you ever had a drink when you first opened your *eyes* in the morning?

When two or more of these questions are answered positively, there is strong indication of a heavy drinking problem.

(b) PHYSICAL DEPENDENCE (SEE CHAPTER 1 FOR SYMPTOMS OF ACUTE WITHDRAWAL AND CHAPTER 10 DIALOGUE 1.)

Time of last drink

State of intoxication

Quantity taken

Associated feelings present, e.g. agitation

Sleeplessness

Other medication

Early morning drinking

Drinking on waking in the night.

(c) MEDICAL INTERVENTION (SEE CHAPTER 7 DIALOGUE 1.)

Examination

It is advisable for drinkers to be checked medically. Some medical aspects of the consequences of drinking may be spotted and clarified to the drinker. This can help in two ways. First, it may relieve an exaggerated anxiety about the 'damage' inflicted. 'If you stay off the drink, your ulcer will have a much greater chance of getting better'. Second, the true nature of a drinking problem may be more simply grasped if put in medical terms. It may help the penny drop. 'You have a tender liver, causing you the pain in your side. I would suggest that is because you are drinking to excess'.

Blood Tests

When considering blood tests as a way of establishing the severity of an alcohol problem, in terms of its physical effects, two tests should be undertaken. Others may be desirable to offer alternative diagnoses. However, the first two tests described below act as an important indicator of alcohol abuse if abnormal results are found and can provide useful, if alarming, information for the drinker:

1. *MCV – Mean Corpuscular Volume*
    Alcohol has a direct effect on bone marrow and this test indicates the size and volume of the red blood cells. If raised in considerable proportion, (normal 90, raised 100+), this is suggestive of heavy drinking. In most cases, it will take three months to return to normal.

2. *GGT – Gamma Glutamyl Transpeptidase*
    This is a liver enzyme and the levels will be raised if the liver is strained or overworked. The GGT rises in order to adapt to the higher levels of alcohol in the blood stream and is raised acutely after a drinking episode.

Normal = 40

Heavy Drinking = 30–100+

If over 100, this can indicate liver damage. GGT levels return to normal in 1 – 2 weeks if drinking stops.

3. *AST – Aspatate Transminase*
   Alcohol causes cell death in the liver and AST is raised due to on-going cell death.

4. *Bilirubin is raised in severe liver impairment*
   Two of these tests together, if abnormal, give a diagnostic accuracy of approximately 80 per cent.

5. Involvement of family and friends

In all assessments, it is important to talk to all family members that are involved with the drinker and are willing to contribute information and experience in order to:

(a) find out what they feel about the drinking (see Chapter 6 dialogue 2).

(b) clarify conflicting perceptions of the same situation with details of drinking (see Chapter 9 dialogue 1).

(c) clarify their involvement in the drinking, i.e., do they drink, themselves? Do they buy drink for their relative? (see Chapter 11 dialogue 1.)

(d) inquire as to their willingness to embark on 'help'.

Discussion with family members needs to be with the knowledge of the drinker. There may be considerable resistance to this. However, given that he knows the drinker better than he knows the other members of the family, the helper can usually gain the trust of the drinker to the extent that the therapeutic alliance will not be too threatened. The family members are, of course, entitled to help in their own right but discussion of where and with whom the most appropriate help is available needs to take place with all concerned and advice may be needed from another colleague for clarification of the most fruitful action.

6. Liaison with other appropriate agencies

Before a complete assessment can be made, it may be necessary to involve other agencies to whom the drinker is known, e.g., GP, psychiatric service, community nursing service, social services. It is important to inform and discuss with the drinker the necessity of such action, in order to maintain the trust within the therapeutic alliance (see Chapter 8 dialogue 1).

If permission is not forthcoming, personal and professional discretion will be needed to assess what will ultimately be most beneficial to the drinker. In the short term, the drinker may see his situation as dangerous and precarious. Experience and supervision may allow the helper to have an overview that may initially seem to be confronting to the drinker, but in the longer term, will bring about change.

The Way Forward

As a means of completing an assessment, the helper and the drinker need to state what has been learnt and understood by both parties. Insights, appraisals and formulations have to be openly shared. It is at this point that some realistic goals can be set that are appropriate to the drinker's situation and needs (see Chapter 6 dialogue 1 and Chapter 10 dialogue 2).

Helper I think that your drinking is more out of control than you had realised.

Drinker Are you telling me that I can't go to the pub?

Helper No, I am saying that we need to find a way of monitoring what you drink so that you can look more closely at what you are doing. I think it would be a good idea to keep a diary of the daily units. What do you think about that?

Drinker That sounds a bit of a fag. What about if I just go out to play darts, three times a week?

Helper That sounds a good idea, although I think you still need to keep an idea of your units. Quantity is what we are concerned with .

Drinker OK, I'll try it.

Once the goals have been set, it is important work to make sure they are adhered to. Drinkers have developed particular defensive systems to cope with their own chaotic emotional worlds – intellectualisation, denial, avoidance, drinking. Life can seem like one big confusion. A sounding board is needed to sort out the 'truth'. The helper, in appropriate settings, needs to provide clearly stated times when she is available to talk. Time-keeping is important to convey limits.

There may be reluctance to abide by the limits set, through lateness, absence, silence. Resistance to help comes into play when therapeutic intervention begins to challenge the defences of an individual. Repressed feelings and experiences re-emerge and block the ability to discuss or recall them. Drinking is the biggest resistance to recovery.

Disclosure of other drug-taking can cause complications, but has to be seen in the same context as drinking unless there is irrefutable medical evidence to suggest otherwise. Family members may attempt to sabotage sobriety. Therapeutic limits may have to be extended to the family to prevent collusion with individual drinking and resistance to change (see Chapter 11 dialogue 1).

Assessments need to continue as the relationship with the drinker progresses. At every meeting, be it daily in a residential setting or weekly at a local group, appraisal can help the drinker pin-point subtle changes. As trust and self confidence build, he can recognise changes within himself and chart the problems and issues that need to be tackled. If the 'family' or those close to him (system) are going through the same process, then real change can be established.

The length of time that such a process will take varies enormously from individual to individual and family to family, and will depend on many different factors. Support and guidance enables the drinker to find personal autonomy and freedom. The helper may need to recognise that she herself is blocking that freedom by promoting undue reliance on the help provided. The helper may have more difficulty 'letting go' than the drinker (see Chapters 3 and 5).

Help may be needed at different points along the journey on which the drinker embarks. Relapse into previous patterns of drinking behaviour may seem the most critical. Without discounting the considerable misery and despair that relapse can produce, most drinkers can acknowledge, with hindsight, that through these times, much can be learnt and understood about what caused the relapse. 'It is not only sadness that makes me drink', a drinker may say. Relapse can be seen as a period of growth if the attitude towards change remains positive and the 'help' is spontaneous and sensitive to the particular situation (see Chapter 10 dialogue 2). When some sense of personal confidence and autonomy begins to return, the type of help offered can be reviewed, changed and even withdrawn.

When an agreed therapeutic time nears completion, an individual may begin to say something important. Is it more helpful to give more time to that person or to stop the session when agreed? Essentially, the helper can only begin to help the drinker create some order out of the emotional chaos he may feel by providing a clearly stated framework. Once the drinker knows the framework, he can begin to decide for himself whether he wants to change. Even through relapse, he can choose whether to remain intoxicated or to seek help. Through his own decisiveness, he can begin to feel his own sense of strength and power to create real change.

To summarise, the helper can be most effective by listening carefully to what the drinker is saying, by gaining an understanding of why such things are being said, and by exploring her own feelings and response to the drinker. The helper must also make a clear assessment with the drinker, as far as is possible, of what the drinker needs, clarify goals and limits that are acceptable to the helper and the drinker and be familiar with the practical help that may be available, i.e., clinics, literature, AA groups, self-help groups. When the demands of the situation stretch beyond those limits, the helper must recognise the need to get further help elsewhere. Help can reduce the chaos and confusion and instill clarity and therefore hope.

CHAPTER 5

'Who Cares About Me?'
Looking After the Helpers

In order for any one person effectively to help another, it is essential to recognise that each of those two people have expectations. If those expectations are not met, there will be a risk of limiting effectiveness. Help may fail, disappointments occur, care can break down and both parties will be affected.

In whatever setting we find ourselves, those of us working with, supporting or living with others who have emotional, physical and often complex problems will need to be aware of our own needs and limitations. We too sometimes have to share our burdens and receive support but all too frequently, there are fears of breaking confidences, of disloyalty and of being seen as not coping – all reasons for doggedly going it alone.

The authors believe that the concept and value of looking after oneself extends to all those who have contact with drinkers – to include the volunteer who comes across drinkers amongst his clients, the social worker who discovers the drinker in the midst of a 'problem family', the worker who chooses to work with drinkers, and to the partners and families of those individuals who use alcohol as a solution to their problems.

It is important that looking after yourself is not seen as a selfish pursuit, but one that can ensure a better quality of care, less worn out workers and a good reputation for the employing organisation. As discussed in Chapter 4 of this book, a better understanding of ourselves, our limitations and our responses can improve our ability to help others.

So, what do we mean when we talk about 'looking after ourselves?' Most of us know, in theory, the importance of a balance of work, rest and play. Likewise, we value the support from within our families, staff group and colleagues. Yet so often it is hard to find these things, to take responsibility for ensuring they happen and to take the risk of confiding in others. Ironically, it is when things are toughest that it can feel most difficult to take advantage of what is on offer and to see where there is a helping hand. It is often said of drinkers: 'If only they would take advice'. It is easier to see that weakness in others.

The kind of help or support needed or desired will mean different things for different people, depending on where they work and where they meet the drinker. In any relationship, it is important to have clear boundaries. We do it as parents, as friends, as siblings and as workers. When those boundaries are in any way violated or abused, that is when relationships can go badly wrong. As the drinker's relationship with alcohol has blurred limits, she may need help in re-establishing not only her own boundaries but some assistance in respecting those of others.

The helper has to face the same issue. Training in the professions places strong emphasis in the code of professional conduct on very clear boundaries between client and worker and the implications of a breach of this conduct can be quite severe. For others, the guidelines are not laid down quite so clearly. However, regardless of how strongly or not they are stated, it does not necessarily make it any easier to get things right.

Once the helper feels able to make an offer of help, he will need to give clear and understandable guidelines to the drinker. She may have been in psychological and emotional chaos for some time.

For example, the helper may say to someone coming to live in a hostel: 'While you are living here, there are two main rules. We ask you not to drink any form of alcohol or take drugs that are not prescribed by a doctor. No damage to persons or property can be tolerated. If these things happen, we will ask you to leave the house' (see Chapter 11 dialogue 2).

It is relatively easy to decide on the 'rules'. It can be far more difficult to stick to them – for both the drinker and helper. What if a resident has just one can of beer? That is a great deal 'better' than the quantity that he is used to. For the helper, it is easy to get drawn into these dilemmas. But is it helpful? Consistency is essential and flexibility desirable but it is crucial that the implications of bending rules are considered before doing so. What is the message if one drink is fine, but two might not be?

Take the example of a mother and her drinking son. If he fails to wake with his alarm and get to work on time, Mum will help. Often parents get drawn into making the phone calls and giving excuses in order to avoid the truth, when 'he is not well today and won't be in' really means 'he had too much to drink last night and can't get up this morning'. No one would wish another to lose a job but this sort of behaviour so easily lets the drinker off the hook, enables him to shift responsibility to someone else so that he can feel safe and actually supported in his drinking.

It is most likely that the parent has been worrying, arguing and talking or even appealing to the drinker to do something about his drinking, yet acts to protect him from the implications of his behaviour. She will inevitably become disappointed exhausted, even exasperated. Whilst the mother's approach is understandable there comes a time when it ceases to be helpful and goes a long way towards helping the drinker maintain his position. The helper may be asking the drinker to keep to the track. Yet as helpers, we find ourselves bending the rules to avoid confrontation, unpleasantness and disagreements. This is one of the hardest aspects of handling drinking problems, yet it is most crucial for change to be initiated.

Co Dependency

The partners of drinkers, after living with them over an extended time, realise that they too have a problem (Mulry 1987). It does not necessarily take the form of alcohol misuse, although this is quite a common occurrence, for people to drink with their partners since life would be intolerable if they did not. Their lives can become dominated by their partner's drinking.

They worry about whether the drinker will keep his job, crash the car on the way home, make a fool of himself in front of friends or embarrass the family. This may go on for so long and reach such a pitch that all their actions, responses and thoughts are taken up and influenced by their drinking partners – 'I can not go out tonight. If I do, she may get drunk whilst I am out'. 'We cannot come this weekend, we are busy', really means, 'I cannot trust Jo not to get very drunk and cause trouble'.

All those whose lives are influenced by that of a drinker are affected, including the partner or colleague who covers up for absence, and the child who does the errands and looks after the siblings because Mum is too drunk. They fear that if they tell something awful will happen. The fusion of boundaries may become so complete and undifferentiated that it may only be an outsider with objectivity and less emotional dependence who can influence and possibly begin to initiate change.

What is of Help to the Helper?

The task of the helper is to seek a clear understanding of the situation. But how can this be done? Support, encouragement advice, information or a place to 'off load' are needed. Clarification of personal actions in relation to what the drinker does or says can help outline a better way forward. Looking at issues raised by the drinker can help identify choices of action and the most appropriate task can be more clearly defined.

To return to the example of the mother and the drinking son – by talking through her situation, she could perhaps see more clearly which action is more helpful to her and her son – to keep telephoning on his behalf, or to take a step back and tell him he will have to do it himself. Such steps take courage. Such steps may create arguments, but those arguments exist already. It may seem that the helper is turning her back on the drinker. By being clear what is the more appropriate course of action can assist with the potential guilt often felt by the helper. Appropriate steps will raise the esteem of the helper and ultimately of the drinker.

Aggressive and volatile behaviour may leave those involved in a state of shock and bewilderment. Sometimes, dealing with the consequences of drinking may be like this (see Chapter 9 dialogue 2). Comfort, quietness, even medical attention may be required. Certainly, a place to talk and share the burden has to be sought to ensure the return of personal esteem.

Falling into the trap of becoming 'over-involved' can, from time to time, affect us all. Identification with the drinker's plight can be creative, empathic and comforting. Many important personal and professional relationships have resulted in a radical change of lifestyle and esteem for the drinker. On the other hand, as discussed in Chapter 4, unrecognised over-identification (or projective identification) can become stifling, undermining and ultimately destructive, particularly for the drinker. In extreme situations, personal and sexual relationships can develop that only contribute to the spiral of emotional chaos that perpetuates drinking.

There needs to be exploration and acknowledgement of feelings, attitudes and behaviour in order that the helper is clear, as far as is possible, about his own actions.

Where to Go for Help

Givers of help may be poor receivers of help. The helper's advice to the drinker may be: 'Find someone to talk to rather than feeling sorry for yourself' and the same applies to the helper. A friend or neighbour may provide an invaluable listening ear, a place to have a chat, get things off one's chest, an opportunity to explore a few suggestions or even to decide upon firm action.

Alcoholics Anonymous, and Al-Anon and Alateen, (the organisations for family and friends of drinkers) provide excellent individual and group support by sharing experiences, fears and dilemmas. It may be beneficial for a partner/friend or professional to attend an AA meeting from time to time, to discover what goes on, how the organisation works and how it gives support to the drinker. However, we believe the non-drinker needs support in his own right. At the Al-Anon meetings, there is opportunity for people to discuss and understand the behaviour of drinkers and, most important, for the individual to explore and understand any contribution he may unwittingly make to that behaviour.

The honesty of these discussions is often remarkable. Self-help groups, local agencies and helplines are all available. Depending on the area, resources will vary. Most can be found in the telephone directory. Personal counselling or therapy for the non-drinker may make a significant difference to the overall behaviour within, for example, a family setting (see Chapter 9 dialogue 1).

For the 'professional', all that has been said applies. To enhance the well-being and progress of the drinker, access to someone to talk through issues raised is vital. As with the relationship with the drinker, the relationship between 'supervisor' and 'supervisee' has to be developed for trust and openness to exist in order that significant work can be done. Expectations of the relationship have to be clearly spelled out, with clear guidelines as to what can be achieved. Support, advice and information are needed. Judgment, fear and intimidation are not.

Frequently, however, the person assigned to supervise is the 'boss' or line manager and then issues of authority, judgment and assessment for promotion may leap into the picture. A sensitive supervisor needs to bear this in mind. For the benefit of good clinical practice, such issues have to be put aside.

Being told what to do without the necessary understanding or information may not bring this about and may re-stimulate issues of authority, whereas open informed discussion is more likely to be beneficial.

The helper asks the drinker to face up to the responsibilities of her behaviour. For effective supervision, the helper needs to ask this of himself. The whole range of human complexities will emerge and a sensitive supervisor will help the supervisee spot what is important in relation to the drinker. It may be, for example, that the helper's poor time keeping, boundary keeping, feelings of frustration, helplessness and fear all need to be explored.

Transference

In Chapter 4, the issue of 'transference' is described as the 'as if' quality that can be assigned, inadvertently or unconsciously to another, when that quality or aspect is not appropriate to the individual. For the purpose of this chapter, it is important to enable the helper to recognise and understand this process. The drinker may see the helper 'as if' she is a punishing parental figure and may react to the 'as if' by, for example anticipating rejection, before getting to know the real strengths of the helper (Hawkins and Shohet 1989). For the drinker, the sense of punishment can feel unbearable. For emotional release the drinker can burden, blame and punish the helper, at times quite fiercely, with comments like 'You are useless at what you do' or This is a complete waste of time'. The intensity of feeling can make the helper feel overwhelmed with those very feelings of uselessness. However, if through the help of a supervisor, he is able to assume the role of the drinker and say (as the drinker): 'I am useless: I feel a complete waste of time', the helper may come to appreciate the extent of the drinker's distress.

Or the drinker may say: 'You are the only person I can talk to'. With such a remark, it is tempting to feel flattered and important to the drinker. However, it is again vital for the helper, with effective supervision, to reverse the projection. What the drinker is really saying may be: 'Please do not leave me' or 'I am so scared of being rejected'. Only if the helper can arrive at these insights can he take the most effective course of action.

Counter-Transference

Without understanding of these interactional processes, the helper can come to feel as battered or as useless as the drinker, a common experience for the drinker's family and friends. As a response, the helper may find himself acting inappropriately or in some way out of character. His behaviour comes as a surprise to him and to those around him. In psychodynamic terms, this would be described as counter-transference (Hawkins and Shohet 1989).

To continue the previous example in which the drinker anticipates rejection, the helper may become snappy, hostile and irritable where previously he had been patient and tolerant. Instead of setting clear limits, he becomes impulsive. He may turn to colleagues to 'support' his decision to stop appointments, block admission. The 'team' or 'system', in turn, becomes entangled in the counter-transference and responds as the drinker initially feared so that once again the vicious cycle of rejection is re-enacted.

In another manifestation of counter-transference, the helper may become very anxious about a drinker, very protective and demanding on his behalf, ringing colleagues for urgent advice and insisting on immediate attention. There are, of course, times when urgency is appropriate and very necessary, but at other times such action can be propelled by an anxiety that is communicated by the drinker and acted on by the helper.

Colleagues, friends, family can become unhelpfully drawn in. Ironically, that initial anxiety or energy may be valuable if the drinker uses it constructively, but if he is allowed to transfer the anxiety, he is left powerless, while others run around 'taking the responsibility'. Very likely, a relationship from the past is being re-enacted. Perhaps his own mother always took control and it is the sense of powerlessness that continues to perpetuate his drinking.

The drinker will carry 'as if' qualities to the relationship with the helper. Likewise, the helper may have similar responses to the drinker. They may appear in ways that are complicated and varied. For illustration, let's take the helper who is continuing to meet with a middle aged woman, in spite of the fact that she continues to drink, is not turning up to appointments and is at times abusive.

With sensitive supervision, it transpires that the helper had a complicated and rejecting relationship with her own mother and is now attempting to 'repair' this through her client. It could be said that the helper is doing a great job in pursuing her client and undoubtedly some very helpful work can be done when allowances are made. However, in this case, there is danger that the helper will become demoralised, 'burn out', and ultimately blame the drinker. This problem is not the drinker's. It belongs to the helper and she is attempting to solve it vicariously and inappropriately through the drinker.

Subtle and complex examples of this process will exist in all personal relationships and will therefore include marriages and partnerships in which drinkers are involved. The important issue is how the complexities within the relationship perpetuate the drinking, for which the drinker alone gets 'blamed' (see Chapter 6 dialogue 2 and Chapter 9 dialogue 1). Help may be needed for each individual within the partnership, or for the couple together to seek help through marital guidance.

Identification with the Drinker

The helper may unconsciously identify in the client some aspect of himself that can only be acknowledged and felt on the other's behalf (projective identification) (Jacobs 1986). Because of this process, the helper's response to the drinker will be affected in some way, depending on how he feels about that aspect of himself. He may be cautious, fearful, overprotective, irritable.

However, creative and empathic relationships are formed within this process and it is only when the identification clouds or distorts the relationship to its detriment that clarification is important.

Take, for example, the helper who is scared to point out that the drinker is not keeping to task. 'I do not want to make him angry as I am scared he will go and drink again'. Perhaps the helper is really saying that he is wary of his own anger and because of this, is preventing his 'client' from experiencing and exploring such feelings for himself. Or consider the example of the helper who continues to see a drinker in spite of clear signs that there is no need. 'I think he still needs my support'. It may well be the helper's problem in separating from a helpful relationship that is being enacted.

Supervision/Support/Befriending

Help for the helper could, therefore, be defined as the provision of a place to talk, to off-load, to understand and identify the processes that exist for us all in all relationships, in order that the helper remain free of the psychological traps in which he can become engulfed. If he remains free, he has more chance of enabling the drinker to become aware of and freed from his habit.

Mirror Images

The drinker can act as a mirror to the helper and, frequently, the material that surfaces in a supervisory setting can reflect what is happening within the relationship with the drinker. The helper may arrive late for supervision, be uninterested in discussion and generally distracted. If this is pointed out, it may transpire that the helper is feeling demoralised. 'Nothing seems to be worthwhile. What is the point? She is only going to drink again'. Some of the 'helplessness' of the drinker is being conveyed by the helper. It needs to be taken back for discussion with the drinker.

Helper   'Do you sometimes feel that nothing is worthwhile?'

Drinker   'Yes! I can't see the point of stopping drinking.'

Helper   'Well, let's look at the benefits of staying sober.'

Drinker   'I suppose I do feel better when I wake up in the morning.'

The supervisor also needs to remember that the forces of transference, countertransference and projective identification that can arise between the helper and drinker can be present between the supervisor and supervisee, especially if the supervisor is in a position of seniority.

Friendships can be founded (and clouded) on these forces too. Although it may not be necessary to identify them as such, friends can sometimes find, to their bewilderment, that they are prepared to 'drop everything' as soon as a drinker telephones. Some understanding of the strength and origin of such reactions may help.

Expectations of Help

All relationships have expectations – two sets. The helper has expectations that the drinker will honour his contract. The drinker, too, has the right to have expectations of the helper. She is entitled to punctuality, privacy, minimised distraction, considered attention and consistency. She deserves respect. Respect enhances self esteem. Creating a model of behaviour can have a powerful effect. Some drinkers have never had this experience.

The helper needs to find the same respect from his source of help. It can be hard to ask for help. Trust and confidence will enable greater freedom. The friend will therefore need to honour his word and be there for six o'clock. The supervisor needs to be punctual and consistent.

Sometimes it is hard to accept that drinkers need not take the helper's advice or opinions. They have the right to choose what they do with their lives. Supervisors/friends need to remind others of this since feelings of helplessness and disappointment usually occur when the helper's expectations of the drinker are not met, and the drinker rejects what is being offered.

Confidentiality

In order to create a place of trust and safety, the issue of confidentiality has to be discussed. Some internal thoughts may be – 'Can I trust you with this information about me?' 'I will feel very disloyal if I tell you that...' Fear of gossip and 'things being held against me' abound. Whilst acknowledging these fears, nobody can prevent another from talking. Conversely everyone can be trustworthy. To clarify the issue, the supervisor/helper/friend may need to say – 'I will not break confidences. However, if there are things that you tell me that trouble me unduly, I may feel obliged to act in some way. You have to be able to trust that I act in your best interest. I will tell you if I think it is necessary to do this and what sort of action I will take'.

When several people are involved with one drinker, in a family or clinical team, all appropriate individuals have to be kept informed of what is relevant. Some information may need to go outside the situation in which the drinker is seen, for example to a general practitioner or health visitor. The drinker needs to be informed and can often see the benefit. Secrets in groups become destructive and intimidating whereas, discretion prevents gossip and fear for all involved. A delicate balance must be maintained.

Working in a Team

For those working within a team whether it be in statutory agencies, voluntary agencies or in families, a consistent approach is important. It is so tempting to be 'the good guy' whilst someone else is the 'bad guy'. It feels good to be the person who can be confided in, who has always got time, who knows just how to make things right. But being in this position can lead to difficulties, for decisions get made in isolation, without consultation. The consequences of these decisions cannot always be supported by one individual alone and further isolation or 'splitting' can occur. Saying 'No' can be hard but colluding confirms the inability of both the drinker and the helper to keep to boundaries.

Another type of inconsistency in a team is allowing one person always to be the one to take on work. If one person is doing this, others cannot. Resentment, competitiveness between colleagues, isolation and collusions arise. Once isolated, people begin to function less effectively and less objectively. Entrenched positions become established and disagreements over the drinker's welfare can ensue. A chaotic, inconsistent approach towards the drinker then mirrors the internal chaos the drinker experiences.

Or, inadvertently, the team may isolate or 'make vulnerable' one of its members. How often is the most junior member of the team allocated to a difficult, demanding situation? How often is the least experienced nurse allocated to a person who requires and indeed needs considerable expertise? Clearly, management tasks need to be completed, but how often is there consideration of the appropriateness of staff allocation, and how often is the issue unconsciously dodged by those who, understandably, do not want to get tangled in a tricky situation? These questions need consideration on two counts: the esteem and strength of the 'junior' and the most effective help for the drinker. Ultimately, the whole team can suffer with disgruntled clients and low self esteem amongst the helpers.

The same behaviour can be observed in families. 'Go and ask your Dad to come home from the pub!' The six-year-old gets to the pub and he is laughed at by Dad's drinking mates. He feels humiliated by them, and feels he has failed his Mum. To whom does he turn? The weakest member of the family has been isolated, made vulnerable. In every family, there are established alliances and relationships even before the problems become apparent. These cannot be ignored. Any problem will highlight the strengths and weaknesses within a relationship. Despite this, the important fact remains that the drinker needs consistency. It is confusing to be told not to drink, that it is causing the family suffering and then to be bought a bottle for a quiet life.

Another illustration of the difficulties of working together is suggested in the example of parents who threaten to throw the drinker out if he returns home drunk again but disagree about whether or not to carry out this painfully difficult task. The son learns that it is only a threat that will not get carried out and so believes that he can continue the same behaviour without fear of action.

Meanwhile, the parents fight about what to do, the drinking behaviour of the drinker does not get addressed and the drinking continues.

Considerations for safe practice

Just as it is important when working with an individual to have clear aims and objectives, this is also true of organisations groups and carers offering help to drinkers. Clear aims objectives and policies enable workers to achieve their task by reducing anxiety, by clarifying boundaries and reducing confusion about what is really expected of them. Policies should be made clear to all workers about how often a helper should discuss his or her case load, or, for example, what should be done if a helper is physically or verbally threatened. Some workers may take aggression in their stride, but it is not helpful to think that everyone should put up with threatening behaviour when others feel frightened and vulnerable. Violence, in any form, is not acceptable.

Whilst we recognise there needs to be room for spontaneity and individual responses to individual clients, it is also true that policy guidelines provide for the safety of helpers and drinkers alike. If the policy states that drinkers should not be seen outside normal working hours when only one person is available in the office, this is for the purpose of protection. It may be the source of enormous frustration and it may be tempting from time to time to ignore the rule but it is a well informed policy and should be adhered to. It isn't that all drinkers are dangerous. It is the recognition that they can be unpredictable, can often arrive intoxicated and can present enormous dilemmas – 'Should he sit there and sober up before he leaves; or, if I turn him away will he just drive off in his car. Then what should I do?'

Helpers will see drinkers in different settings. The social worker or community nurse may need to visit a client at home.

Estranged couples may agree to meet to attempt reconciliation. It may be helpful for someone to know where the helper is going, to know her movements for the day and to be aware of any anxieties she might have about her meeting or appointment. Take an escort if concerns are high. If this is not possible, then it may be advisable to re-think the venue. A health centre may be more appropriate than a house visit and a café more suitable than the home.

It would be wrong to convey a sense that all meetings with drinkers are risky but it is also unhelpful not to respond to intuitive feelings about a situation. Helpers are only human. There are no rewards for coping alone. If they are feeling anxious, they may convey a sense of feeling unsettled to the drinker. This is unhelpful since his sense of chaos is often finely balanced by his belief that the helper is in control. If this proves not to be the case, an insecure and unsafe atmosphere may result.

A GP may not know until a patient is in his consulting room whether or not his patient is intoxicated. If a patient is known to have a problem, has arrived previously intoxicated and been verbally aggressive, a different approach to that individual may be called for. Why not consider calling the client from the waiting room oneself and meeting the client before the consulting room door is shut? A decision could then be made to involve another person, leave the door open or just tell a colleague that you may need assistance. The drinker will feel safer too. In this way you have planned for support or help should assistance be needed.

Everyone's safety and that of their environment needs to be considered. Refusing to see a patient may not be possible although in certain situations this may be considered advisable. A general hospital cannot turn people away who are asking for help. Equally they should be clear that they are responding to clinical evidence and not to threats when they make a decision for intervention or admission. Again, clear guidelines need to be discussed, documented and easily available to reduce the anxiety of potential unpredictability.

In a residential setting, for example, an intoxicated individual can be asked to sleep off her drunkenness and then asked to leave. Or two members of staff will be clearly designated to escort the individual off the premises while alerting the whole team of the situation. Preventing too many people getting involved reduces panic and fear for the drinker. Give the drinker enough space so that he does not feel cornered. In more isolated settings with fewer staff, designate a quiet but not separate space where an interview can take place uninterrupted. There is no harm in asking for help and be aware of where that help is available at all times. Effective management of any situation will undoubtedly increase.

Drinking and Driving

Driving with a blood alcohol level of over 80mg/100ml is against the law. It is dangerous to oneself and others to drive a car in this condition. How often does a drinker inform a helper that he is about to drive away? How often do friends leave intoxicated and we wave them goodbye with a cheerful smile? Perhaps there is a cursory 'I hope that he does not get copped' or 'I hope he will get home safely'. The consequences of drinking and driving are hideous, yet intervention is rare (see Chapter 1).

If the drinker weeps about her uncontrollable urge to hurt her children, the helper may need to act. Such information may have to be discussed with relevant agencies for the protection of her children. Yet there is little intervention when a heavily intoxicated individual leaves a hospital or house with the intention of driving a car.

If we know that someone has been drinking and is about to drive, as citizens, we have a moral obligation to point out the risks that that person is putting herself and others in. If we are told this information in confidence, or within the bounds of a professional relationship, what should we do?

We believe our prime responsibility in this situation is to the clients, or drinkers. We must try as hard as possible to dissuade them from doing so. We can talk with them, suggest alternatives – get a taxi, ask someone to collect them, allow them to wait until the effects of the drink have worn off (see Chapter 9 dialogue 2).

Should these persuasions fail, the question of involving the police is raised. The dilemma is whether or not it will truly assist the drinker in dealing with his problem if this dimension is added. Our aim is to get alongside the drinker and not to make him feel alienated. Yet he is putting himself and others at risk.

Betraying professional confidences is permissible in given situations 'to act in the public interest' (British Association of Occupational Therapists 1990). Most professionals have a code of conduct to which they may refer. For us all, the difficulty arises in our willingness or ability to assess accurately the extent of the danger involved. Whilst we know that alcohol impairs judgment, what would be our criteria for intervention? Within well established relationships, successful intervention may be easier than with someone we know less well.

Each helper will have to be guided by his own experience in the assessment of the individual involved. Whatever the decision, it is helpful to have, if possible, another person present to witness any discussion. Policy guidelines that are well discussed, informed and disseminated must play a vital role in this crucial issue (British Medical Association 1988). Discussion with police, employers, local agencies, even politicians to create a consensus for appropriate action will enable all of us to take a step nearer to safe-guarding the lives of drinkers and others.

Alcohol policies – the work place

Complications arise when the consequences of an individual's drinking affect work performance. Lateness, unreliability and absenteeism can only be tolerated for so long (see Chapter 8 dialogue 2). Resentments and frustrations emerge, gossip and secrets abound yet no-one dares to intercept.

In the past, the normal attitude to drunkenness or the consequences of drinking behaviour at work would depend on the status of the individual involved. It could vary from collusion to dismissal. In recent years there has been a move to formalise work place policies to enable the individual who is drinking to receive help. At the same time, the employing organisation can expect a commitment to the job by the drinker seeking help.

The issue of alcohol use and misuse may be one aspect of any policy which usually includes other health issues such as smoking, exercise, stress, nutrition. Such policies should be drawn up and made available to all employees. The knowledge that such a policy exists should enable the drinker to seek help without fear of punishment. Colleagues can stop any cover-up and collusion over another's drinking and have a clear understanding of the appropriate action to be taken.

Drinking, while at work, to say farewell or to celebrate, is common practice. However, its appropriateness must always be questioned. Talking to drinkers while smelling of alcohol is not acceptable practice and to encourage colleagues to over-indulge is breaking professional conduct. Judgment is severely affected by alcohol.

It is important that there should be established policies which give clear instructions to occupational health, personnel officers, foremen, line managers, amongst others regarding drinking at work. Such established policies avoid individual or punitive responses and provide a consistent and ultimately 'helpful' approach. Suggestions for deciding and implementing a policy for drinkers can be found in the literature listed below:

Danger! Drugs at Work. An Employee's Guide to Drug Use. (1986) London: Confederation of British Industry.

Cyster, R., Macklin, D. and McEwen, J. (1987) Alcohol Policies: a Guide to Action at Work. London: The Industrial Society.

The Post Office (1986) 'Someone Like You' (training package video) London: The Post Office.

Robert, R., Cyster, R. and McEwen, J. (1988) Alcohol Consumption and the Work Place: Prospects for Change. Public Health 103: 463–469.

Training for the Helpers

Very often the helper struggles to keep up with the recently published literature that discusses new thinking and differing attitudes to drinking problems. In service training can be of enormous value. Attending conferences and lectures offers an opportunity to meet other people and exchange ideas which enables us to feel differently about our work. To discuss ideas and exchange views is essential for the maintenance of a fresh approach.

In service training can vary in quality and quantity. It is important that case review takes place regularly so that where possible other disciplines may be included, since the bringing together of experience can be enormously beneficial to learning and practice.

For the family member, relative or friend, attendance at Al-Anon or Alateen can provide enormous support, learning and sharing of a problem that can at times feel insurmountable. Alcohol advisory lines, self help groups, Alcohol Concern are all there to be used. There are many books available offering information on health education. A list is provided at the end of this book.

Conclusion

Self help in all forms is not only about a commitment to oneself but can and should be seen very much as an investment for the 'unit' or place in which you meet the drinker, be it your family, your church, your work place or your organisation. The drinker will ultimately be the beneficiary.

CHAPTER 6

'Early Warning' – The First Signs

Dialogue 1. Interview with Counsellor in a General Practice

Scene

Adrian James, a young man of 19, has been sent to see his GP as his mother is worried about him. She says he seems rather listless, spending considerable time away from home, and when he is at home, he spends a lot of time on his own or asleep. She is also concerned that, from time to time, she finds he has a wet bed. The GP confirms a rather dull, listless picture and asks Adrian to go to talk to the Counsellor (Jane) attached to the practice. Below is an account of that conversation.

JANE	Hello, come in Mr James, please take a seat. I am Jane Thomas. Thank you for coming along this morning. I hope through this interview we might both gain an understanding of what is going on for you. Where would you like to start?	*Respect for client important. He will feel nervous and bewildered. Opening statements from both sides are important for setting the scene for productive discussion.*
ADRIAN	My doctor suggested I come along. My Mum's been worrying again.	*Feels a mixture of concern and reluctance. He managed to attend the appointment. Seems rather controlled by others.*
JANE	Worrying about you?	*Reflect back what he is saying and focus on Adrian.*
ADRIAN	Yes, well, she always has someone. It used to be my Dad and he died quite recently. Before that it was my Gran, and before that – well, she always worries.	*Perhaps Adrian is describing the 'system' by which this family deals with its concerns (see Chapter 2). Adrian is now the focus of that system. Be alert to whose problem is being presented. Is Mum's*

worry something he denies/ignores/resents, or is it a way of gaining something for herself?

JANE   Why should your mother be worrying about you?

Clarify if he sees a need for her to worry. He has come to the interview.

ADRIAN   She got me to go along to the doctor. I'd been having this problem since my Dad got sick, but she didn't really bother then. Since he died, she's been on at me to do something.

Does acknowledge that he has a problem, but presenting it as mother's worry. Is he caught by the need of the family to have an identified person to worry about? The only way to get close to Mum is to have a problem. He is feeling confused and uncertain and obviously describing some stress, not only now but also about his father. Is he grieving for his father? Talker needs to remain open-minded as to the cause of the bedwetting. It is not yet clear what problem he is describing. Help him towards this.

JANE   I know that your GP thinks there is a difficulty, as he sent me a letter. How do you see the situation?

It might be tempting to tackle the problem as seen by others before getting a clear understanding of how he sees things. There is a risk of losing the client if the talker follows the pattern of those around him (i.e., mother) and gets pulled into the 'system'. It is therefore important he makes a self-assessment, without which he will not be able to identify his own goals.

ADRIAN   It has not been too bad since I saw the doctor. It's only happened twice.

Beginning to make assessment, yet not able to say what IT is. Feels very fearful and confused as to what his problem is. Talker must be sensitive to this and think carefully before asking the next question. Interview feels sticky.

JANE   I'm glad you see that things are better. I am wondering how they are different?

Important to recognise change. Going with fear without confrontation, respecting the continuing difficulty of the subject matter.

ADRIAN Don't know.

Feels confused as so much has happened. May also feel trapped and embarrassed.

JANE   OK, let's go back to the beginning when you said your Mum was worried. What do you need to do to stop her worrying about you?

Help remove the sense of confrontation and being trapped; but important to keep the focus. Leave some responsibility with him.

ADRIAN I think if I could stop it, she'd be happier.

Beginning to see he may be responsible for some of her worries, and therefore is beginning to engage with the interview.

JANE   Are you referring to the same problem as your doctor mentioned in his letter to me? He says you have been waking in a wet bed some mornings.

Be gentle with this information. But it is unhelpful to let Adrian struggle too long to find his own words.

ADRIAN Well, that only happens when I have been out with friends.

Is he suggesting that the bed wetting is not the whole story? Be open to what he is saying.

JANE   Can you tell me any more?

State your openness, although he may find this frightening.

ADRIAN Don't really know.

Finds it difficult to respond.

JANE   Where do you go with your friends?

Needing more direction – may be a clue as to the role Mum plays in his life (see Chapter 4).

ADRIAN We go to the pub, usually.

Spontaneous, undefended statement. Almost a relief from the heaviness of the moment.

JANE	And what happens there?	*Begin to explore his attitudes.*
ADRIAN	We have a few beers, and a bit of a laugh.	*Feels happier in that environment.*
JANE	And you have noticed yourself that if you have been out with friends, you are more likely to wet the bed.	*Help him to recognise that he has the information which can help him to understand what is going on.*
ADRIAN	Did I? Don't know really.	*Reluctant to return to look at difficulties.*

The conversation has reached an important stage. What is Adrian's real concern and, therefore, what help is he asking for? Adrian has alluded to the connection between his bedwetting and his visits to the pub, although he has probably not acknowledged that they could be connected. The talker knows that Adrian has recently lost his father and his bedwetting may be a consequence of that loss. However, the talker needs to be open to wider issues, including drinking, without making Adrian too frightened. To put the issue of drinking to one side may be more the avoidance of the talker than the client or drinker (see Chapters 3 and 4). It may be helpful to keep the exploration in the context that the issues have been presented.

JANE	So, how can you help your mother stop worrying?	
ADRIAN	She's not keen on my friends. Um... I'm never around at mealtimes and I'm often late home, when I'm not working.	*Mother feels out of control and is doing the worrying or controlling for him, which leaves him unconnected to his own responsibilities. Mother is having to struggle with loss of husband at the same time as her son needs to separate from her. Is he failing to live up to unspoken expectations – i.e., a man about the house, a companion for her.*
JANE	Are these the friends you go to the pub with?	*Help him to connect with what he has said, to clarify the picture.*
ADRIAN	Yeah, we meet there, play darts, mess about.	

JANE	So what is it that worries your Mum about that?	*Was Dad a drinker? Is history repeating itself? Return to this subject later on. Is there some displacement of worry going on? (see Chapter 2.)*
ADRIAN	Well, I get late for work. She can't get me up in the morning.	*May be rebelling against her need to control him, but he is not facing his own responsibilities.*
JANE	Is anyone else getting at you?	*Does his behaviour affect anyone else?*
ADRIAN	Yes, work. I've had a few warnings about my lateness. I've been told it will have to improve.	*Feels pressure from all sides.*
JANE	So, you might lose your job unless things change? What do you think needs to change?	*Things look fairly serious. More clues as to the possible extent of his drinking. Needs some help to make connections.*
ADRIAN	Don't know.	*Unable to understand.*
JANE	As you have suggested, perhaps this is connected with being out late with your friends.	
ADRIAN	Could be.	*Beginning to reflect.*
JANE	Can you tell me a little bit about your work and your family?	*Help him to say as much or as little as he wants.*

The talker establishes that Adrian is the middle of three children. He is of average intelligence but left school without exams. He never felt much encouragement to do well so he believes he didn't try as hard as he might have. He left school about 18 months ago. His father died after a six month illness shortly after Adrian had left school and had started working in a factory. He works long hours, mostly at night. He has little contact with the rest of the family, although his younger brother is still living at home.

His father was hard on him, called him 'devious' and 'untrustworthy', so they were not close. His father drank in the pub with friends and at times would encourage his son to join him but would ridicule him publicly. He was not able to talk much with him when he was ill and feels a sense of relief that he is not around, although he feels very guilty about this. He feels quite close to his mother but finds her rather unpredictable.

From the history ascertained, there are problems surrounding Adrian's relationship with his recently deceased father. There is a suggestion that alcohol is involved in some way. For the purposes of this chapter, the conversation below can serve to illustrate how the effects of alcohol can be assessed and made relevant to the overall picture of Adrian's difficulties.

JANE   So, your father drank in the pub?

ADRIAN   Well, he sometimes came home smelling of booze.

JANE   I would like to ask you about what I call lifestyles.

Allows exploration not only centred on alcohol, giving a wide picture of attitudes, self esteem and external pressures (see Chapter 2).

         Are you a smoker?

ADRIAN   Yes, though I should give it up. I think it finished my Dad off.

There will always be issues raised by clients which cannot be responded to at the time. It is important to acknowledge them and come back to them later if appropriate.

JANE   That sounds important. Can we talk about your father in a moment? Have you tried to stop smoking?

ADRIAN   No, not really.

JANE   I think that you know there are serious consequences to smoking and if you can stop, your health would certainly benefit. What do you smoke?

ADRIAN   Benson and Hedges... about fifteen a day.

JANE   And what about things other than tobacco.

ADRIAN   What do you mean?

Feels a little alarmed.

JANE	Do you smoke pot?	*Important to find out about other drug use (see Chapter 4).*
ADRIAN	Well, I have but I don't now.	
JANE	Do you have any medicines from your doctor?	
ADRIAN	Nothing regularly.	
JANE	How about other things not from your doctor?	
ADRIAN	No, I wouldn't touch them. There's enough about but they're not for me.	*Clear about limits.*
JANE	What about drink? You say you go to the pub with friends. What do you drink?	
ADRIAN	Beer, mainly.	
JANE	And when did you have your first drink?	*It may be tempting to ask how much he drinks straight away. This may be too confrontative and may feed denial. Asking about the progression of drinking can give the drinker and the talker a clearer idea of how things have developed.*
ADRIAN	13, 14.	
JANE	Where was this? At home or with friends?	*Is he with a peer group or in isolation?*
ADRIAN	With friends. We all did it.	*Is there pressure to join the group? (see Chapter 2)*
JANE	Can you remember how often you drank in the week?	*What was the extent of the drinking?*
ADRIAN	Once, maybe twice a week.	
JANE	And did you ever get drunk?	*Was there loss of control?*
ADRIAN	A bit silly.	*Normal adolescent experiments.*

JANE	What did you drink then?	*What may be appropriate to his age and stage?*
ADRIAN	Cider, in the fields.	
JANE	That was about five years ago now. How do you think things have changed?	*Help him make his own assessment of his 'journey'.*
ADRIAN	Well, I drink beer – in the pub.	
JANE	How often might you go to the pub? Last week, for instance?	*Clarify his drinking pattern.*
ADRIAN	I didn't go out so much last week because, as I say, my job is a bit dodgy being late so many times.	*Feels a bit cagey about answering this. Suggests some guilt about excesses but beginning to recognise limitations.*
JANE	When you do go out, how much might you drink?	*Don't be put off. It is important for both parties that the issue is neither shied away from or becomes 'worried about'. That is the family pattern (see Chapters 2 and 4).*
ADRIAN	I have a few beers.	
JANE	What do you call a few beers?	
ADRIAN	Don't know. It could be ten pints, it could be three. Depends on the company and money and when the pub is going to close.	*Drinking responding to social limits, but going over personal capacity.*
JANE	So, a typical week might be…? Any lunch time drinking?	*Ascertain a picture of overall consumption.*
ADRIAN	When I finish early shift at 1pm, we go to the pub till about 3pm. I'd may be have five pints. Then I'd go out on Friday and Saturday with friends and drink ten pints or so.	

JANE	That helps me to see that there might be some pattern to your drinking. Do you think your drinking gives you any problems?	
ADRIAN	No, not really, just late for work sometimes.	*Acknowledging some insights.*
JANE	You mentioned earlier that there might be a link between going out with your friends and having a wet bed the next morning.	*Feed back what you have heard him say and that he may, for whatever reason, not want to focus on.*
ADRIAN	That is what my Mum worries about.	*Not able to acknowledge this possible connection yet. Perhaps Mum carries some of his worries.*

This is where the interview first began and it seems that the family patterns are firmly set and too complex to tackle in the first interview. Furthermore, the drinking may be intrinsically tied up in that family pattern (see Chapter 2). However, it is important for Adrian and Jane to clarify how much the drinking is involved in the pattern, to prevent it becoming too entrenched at this early stage. This could be done as follows:

JANE	I have some information here that tells you about safe limits of drinking. Those limits are defined by looking at the quantity of drink in units of alcohol. Let's look at it – and perhaps you could add up your units.	*See Chapter 1.*
ADRIAN	It comes to 50 if I drink what I just said. But last week I had about 20.	*Feeling defensive*
JANE	Do you think that is OK?	*Allow him to make his own assessment so that he does not feel trapped.*
ADRIAN	Well, it's OK. Doesn't affect me much.	

JANE	Right now you are fairly fit and healthy. However, there are recommendations about how much alcohol is safe over a long period. You seem to be well above those limits at times and just within them at others.	*Be clear with the facts. He needs to know them in order to help him bring about some understanding of his behaviour and therefore some change.*
ADRIAN	They seem quite low to me. Most people I know drink much more than that.	*Still feeling defensive. Finding it difficult to take responsibility for himself.*
JANE	I realise you may not drink every day. But it seems that when you do, there are consequences that are unpleasant for you that could well be linked to that amount.	*Help clarify clear goals that are mutually acceptable. This can instill hope.*
JANE	I suggest you keep a diary over the next week of what you drink, where you do your drinking and how it affects you. What do you think about that idea?	
ADRIAN	All right, I'll give it a try.	
JANE	We can make another appointment and we can go through it together.	
ADRIAN	OK but you won't tell my Mum, will you? She'll only worry.	*The core of the problem returns.*
JANE	I respect your need for privacy and it is up to you what you want to tell your mother. It might be important to include her at some stage, but when will depend on you. Here are some leaflets with information about alcohol and we can meet discuss your diary next week.	*Important to help Adrian to remember the whole picture so that all aspects of his situation can be addressed when he is ready.*

A diary can help the drinker to understand more clearly the effects of his drinking. In the case of Adrian, he may discover that there is a clear link between excess drinking and bedwetting. However, it may become clear to the drinker and to the talker that the drinking may have exacerbated the bedwetting but also there remains an underlying cause, perhaps grief for his father, with which he is struggling and with which he would need further help. It is only through the clarification of the effects of alcohol that such an assessment can be made.

Dialogue (2) Conversation Between Husband and Wife

Scene

David, 54, is a manager in a large firm. He is over-committed to his job and works long hours. Joan, 50, has no paid employment outside the home and is very involved in local affairs. They have two children who have left home.

Both parties in this dialogue are intrinsically and emotionally involved. Because of the problem of describing a process that is applicable to both parties, statements printed in the 'process' column are comments that would otherwise not be made and are perhaps hidden by the words used.

JOAN	Are you coming to bed David?	*I would like to spend some time with you.*
DAVID	I'll just have a nightcap and follow you up.	*Perhaps I get more comfort from a drink.*
JOAN	David, I am really concerned about your health: I don't think you are as fit as you used to be.	*I feel excluded. I also feel worried about where this is leading us. I can't be as direct as I would like to be.*
DAVID	Well, nobody is as fit as they were when they were teenagers – responsibilities and the daily grind doesn't give you the opportunity for exercise and sport like you have when you are a youngster.	*I feel guilty and defensive but I am feeling careworn and need some understanding.*
JOAN	I'm not really talking about exercise so much, David. I'm getting worried about how much harm you might be doing to yourself through (*nods at glass*)... through that!	*I feel I must make my point. I don't want to miss (avoid) the opportunity again.*

DAVID   I wouldn't worry about that. I never get pissed nowadays like I used to. I remember I used to drink much more when I was a student.

I need to try and console her and myself.

JOAN   But was it every night?

Help, this may have been going on longer than I realise.

DAVID   Well, maybe it was not every night, but it was most nights.

Help, perhaps I have not been honest with myself or others.

There is a point of connection here that they are both thinking but are unable to communicate to each other: 'this drinking has been going on for a long time and we both need to realise that'. The next statement reveals some acknowledgement of the dependency on alcohol.

JOAN   You never have a night without a drink now. You seem to need it.

I feel scared, helpless and out of control.

DAVID   No, I don't need it. It's just that it helps me relax because I find it's very stressful at the office, and I need to wind down.

I feel scared too – too scared to acknowledge it. I feel pressure from within and from everywhere outside.

Both Joan and David feel scared and out of control and neither can express this directly. This perhaps contributes to drinking.

JOAN   Well, David, I AM worried. I cleared out the house for the dustmen yesterday. It is only a week since I did it last and there were three empty scotch bottles – and there have been two or three every week for quite a long time now.

I'm scared because I know what is going on.

DAVID   Oh, stop getting at me. I'm tired! Let's go to bed.

I know you know and I feel very small. I also feel worn out by all the stress. I feel persecuted and unable to explain myself.

JOAN	David, I am not getting at you, I am just worried about it. I'm just worried for your sake. It's not some thing we have ever talked about before. I'm sure it is more than is good for you and it seems to be getting worse.	*I find this as hard to talk about as you. I need to talk about it. I am not sure what else I can do.*

Here is a good example of how the drinker can be given the responsibility of changing his behaviour, but in fact there is a mutually shared feeling of fear and helplessness.

DAVID	Look, shut up will you? Message received. I'll hide the bottles or throw them away myself in future. Do you want me to turn into a secret drinker?	*I feel more bottled up than ever now. Don't give me all the pressure or else we can not reach each other at all.*
JOAN	I'm just really frightened. You never used to get angry like this. It has been going on for weeks now; you're very irritable and not very talkative (bursts into tears).	*I must say this as I can't take the strain of 'bottling things up'.*
DAVID	(pauses a moment). Oh I'm sorry I lost my temper. I do feel I am under a lot of stress at the moment and I am sure it will get a lot better when they sort out the new management structure at work. Please bear with me, and I'll try and remember what you told me. Now let's go to bed and not get too upset.	*Oh God, I feel fairly desperate, but I can't let her or myself know how bad I am feeling.*

Both parties are able to share some vulnerability and some of their respective emotional positions. However, both are maintaining their individual protection against the pain of the situation – Joan, by misplacing responsibility onto David for 'drinking' and David by rationalising away the burden and responsibility. It is at the intervention of a third party that can clarify and dislodge such defences.

| JOAN | All right, but just one last thing, and I promise I will not say any more after that. | *I am not sure that I want to know how bad you are feeling and I need to say when things are too much for me.* |

Joan would like to look after David but cannot give him the comfort for which he strives (see Chapter 3)

DAVID	What do you want to say?	*I want to keep trying to be open.*
JOAN	If I am worried again, will you let me talk to you without you losing your rag? Please – because I do worry.	*I find your anger very hard to cope with.*
DAVID	Yes, yes, all right Joan, I promise.	

The last part of the dialogue demonstrates the dilemma of who in fact, in a relationship, holds the emotional control and highlights the difference in how that control is expressed. For the drinker it will be through alcohol. For the partner, that expression is less obvious but equally powerful.

Ten days later...

JOAN	Welcome home, dear. Have you had a hard day – you are late.	*I want to greet him, but I am furious he is so late.*
DAVID	Well, I had a drink with two or three of the people from the accounts department whose jobs are on the line. They're in a bad way, trying to drown their sorrows. I had to go, really.	*I will tell her straight.*
JOAN	I hope you have not had too much yourself. Don't forget you have already been caught for drunk driving.	*If I can't control him, perhaps the police can.*

Joan is having difficulty acknowledging her own sense of feeling out of control and she focuses it on the drinking and the drinker.

| DAVID | I have only had two pints, over two hours, and I know when I am fit to drive. | *I feel in control but you do not trust me or my own self control. You want the control for yourself.* |

The issue of control may be reminiscent of former relationships and can eventually perpetuate increased drinking.

| JOAN | Do you remember our little agreement a fortnight ago? | *I don't feel I can trust you. See, you can't look after yourself.* |

Joan is slipping into a parental role which David is unconsciously seeking.

| DAVID | But I have been trying. Haven't you noticed how few empties there are now? | *I have been trying… to placate you. I feel very small, in the child role.* |
| JOAN | But you have been going to the pub instead. | *I feel you have been trying to avoid me.* |

Joan feels punitive, perhaps in response to David's retreat into a childlike position.

| DAVID | We need to look after each other; things are getting very heavy. | *I want to make a go of this together. This is a joint problem.* |

David is trying to alter the interaction and take some of the responsibility.

| JOAN | I am trying to look after you. | *You don't seem to appreciate what I am trying to do.* |

Joan is resisting the attempt to shift the interaction as it is too scary and would necessitate a relinquishing of some control.

DAVID	I know you are, dear, but as I keep saying, these are difficult times at the moment and it should all be sorted in a month or two.	*I will have to keep reassuring you and myself.*
JOAN	OK, I know you are under a lot of pressure, but I've had an idea that will be good for both of us.	
DAVID	Oh, what's that?	
JOAN	Well, it's Lent in two weeks. Perhaps we could both give up something. I was thinking that I need to lose some weight so I'll give up sweets if you give up	

drinking at home during the
week. Is that a fair deal, so we
can do something together that
is good for us both?

DAVID   All right, as long as it doesn't
stop me going out and I can
have one or two with the lads.

JOAN   It's a deal. Just for Lent. And we
will buy each other presents if
we succeed. Then we can
celebrate!

The end of the dialogue shows an attempt to alter the balance of interaction, but
Joan is maintaining the control and responsibility because it is her suggestion.
These contracts seldom work as the drinker has not initiated the change and is
still in a position of placating his partner.

Ten days into Lent...
David arrives back from work looking fraught and is restless; he is unable to
read or watch TV. He pours himself a large scotch in full view of Joan.

DAVID   What are you looking at me like   *I feel swamped and defeated.*
that for? I've had a bloody day
at work – I've never felt under
so much stress.

David is surrounded by punishing figures everywhere. He cannot please any
of them, not even his wife. He is not sufficiently emotionally resilient to be
objective to these forces (see Chapters 3 and 4).

JOAN   But what about... Lent?   *But what about... us... and me?*

DAVID   Oh stuff Lent. I need a drink.   *'We' don't matter as 'we' cannot*
You can't stop me, you know.   *work for 'me'.*

Perhaps both Margaret and David are expressing their own different sets of
needs, that are in competition with each other.

JOAN   Life is getting very difficult in   *We can't seem to reach each other.*
this house. There is always an   *I feel angry with you for not taking*
atmosphere when you come   *care of me!*
home and I don't feel we are
close anymore.

DAVID   Oh… don't give me that. It's   *I feel guilty, angry and trapped. I*
emotional blackmail. I'm fed up   *can't be with you and I can't even*
with you wingeing at me.   *be with myself.*
Nobody's perfect and a lot of
them are much worse than I am
at the moment.

angry silence.

DAVID   Oh, I'm sorry; there I go again.
But I'm sure that being able to
relax has helped me to keep my
job while others have lost theirs.

David is facing a confused reality. How much does alcohol help and how much does it hinder? It is true that he is maintaining his job, but his 'stress' is focused on his work and not on himself. Yet he is medicating himself with alcohol.

JOAN   Oh, but what is it doing to you?
What is it doing to us?

Joan is also facing a tangled reality. She does not know what to respond to – the drinking, the stress or the difficulties they have together at home. However, the focus remains on the drinking.

DAVID   I told you, it's because it is a   *And my focus will remain on the*
stressful time; it looks like things   *stress of work.*
are getting better now.

JOAN   I think people should be able to   *I think we need some help.*
get help with dealing with that
sort of awful stress.

DAVID   Yes, but that's what families are   *I need you to stand by me.*
for.

JOAN   But doctors can recognise how   *I am not sure I can manage your*
        much harm stress can do, and I   *stress as I find it hard to manage*
        saw Dr Watkins at the surgery   *my own.*
        the other day about my
        headaches. He was really
        helpful; he understands why
        people feel like they do, and I
        am sure he'd be able to give you
        some advise about stress and
        things. And he could give you a
        check over to see that your
        health is not coming to any harm.

DAVID   Hmmmmm...

JOAN   If you do that, I'll be much   *It will be a relief if someone else*
        happier. Will you agree, please,   *can look after you for a little while.*
        for my peace of mind as well?

DAVID   Oh, all right.

JOAN   I'll phone the surgery in the
        morning.

Joan continues to take the initiative for David, and he continues to want to please her. For these reasons, David may not be able to respond as the search for change is not coming from him at present. However, Joan's actions may precipitate him into getting help which may lead to some clarification towards where the problems lie. These not only rest with the drinking. They rest with the two individuals' interaction and their attitude to drinking. They may choose to seek help together or individually, through counselling, Alcoholics Anonymous, or Al Anon. Until such time as attitudes are changed, the drinking is unlikely to diminish.

CHAPTER 7

'What, Me?' – Detection and Prevention

Dialogue (1) Consultation with General Practitioner

Scene

A 38-year-old man, Tom, has been troubled by sickness and stomach pain for several months now. He feels worried and scared and is unable to look at his health as a whole, focusing principally on his stomach problem. He has been keen to get help from his GP, Dr Palmer, for the pain. The following dialogue may illustrate the difference in expectations of 'help'.

From the results of the blood tests (see Chapter 4) Dr Palmer has a strong indication that alcohol abuse may be at the root of Tom's problems. However, this is a long way away from how Tom sees things. He has acknowledged that he has a few beers from time to time and sees no problem with his alcohol consumption. He does, however, come repeatedly for help with his gastric and emotional 'pain'.

TOM	Morning doctor, I've come for the results of my blood tests.	*Feels fairly confident that things will be sorted out. Fed up with feeling so down.*
DR P	Oh, yes, now let me see, we were trying to get to the bottom of this sickness and stomach ache you've been having.	*Make him feel at ease, and meet him at his perception of the problem. Tom is very scared and could easily run away if care is not taken. Step slowly, because he needs to be informed of the truth.*
TOM	Yeah, I don't know what they were for. I need to get this sorted because it's getting me down really – and you're the doctor...	*Feels an urgent need for an answer. Feels confused and asking for direction. 'I need you to look after me.'*

Tom is asking for help but denying the real problem. Furthermore, he is investing considerable reliance on 'the doctor' to help him. In society, doctors are commonly seen as 'the one who can make it right'. The fear that this will not be achieved may be acute and can directly mirror past events in the drinker's history (see Chapter 3).

For the talker, both the denial and the overt helplessness of the drinker can create feelings of impatience, irritation, even punitiveness, especially if there is a sense that the drinker will not listen and 'he is wasting my time'. Such feelings may emerge to prevent the talker from feeling overwhelmed by the drinker's neediness, or as a defence against his own issues. 'I can't help this man with all he wants' (see Chapter 4). What is important is that these feelings do not become enacted against the drinker. Likewise, the drinker has to start to recognise what he really needs.

DR P	Mmm, let's have a look. As I thought, there are a few things that aren't quite right – well, three, actually.	*It would be easy to remain protective. Need to find a way for Tom to translate the facts in a way that he can accept. Don't rush. His stomach is unable to digest what is happening.*
TOM	What do you mean, 'not quite right'? Is it serious?	*Feels anxious. He knows it is serious but is scared or unable to acknowledge this himself.*
DR P	Well, one of them is about your blood cells, which are a bit too big and the others are to do with your liver and pancreas. Before I go on to explain them, what do you think these blood tests might have shown?	*Be clear with the facts and help Tom to begin to come to his own understanding, as this will be less scary than being 'told'.*
TOM	I don't think I even thought about it – I just thought you were sorting out my stomach pains and my sickness. I suppose they might tell you if I've got an ulcer or something like that.	*Beginning to accept some responsibility for his problem, but still needing to 'pin' it onto something physical as a way of backing off from his distress.*
DR P	I am wondering if you were worried about something quite serious?	*Try and help him not to back off.*
TOM	What do you mean? It's not... it's not.. no, young blokes like me don't get... cancer.	*Indicates how much worry he is carrying but how he misdirects his concern with his own denial.*

DR P	No it is certainly not cancer, but it *is* something we need to take seriously.	*Dispel the fantasies, but need to work with the concern as he may not be ready to 'hear' the truth – his denial may be too entrenched. Likewise the talker may not be ready to speak the truth for fear of the drinker's response.*
TOM	What – you mean it is an ulcer.	*'I can handle that'.*
DR P	Well, blood tests can't show ulcers in your stomach, but they can give an idea if there is something that might be causing an ulcer or other stomach problems.	*Start to build the jigsaw.*
TOM	Like something wrong with my blood or an infection, or something like that? What is it?	*He is angry and feeling denied and frightened.*
DR P	Well, your blood cells and your liver and pancreas are being poisoned. The blood tests show how they are struggling to neutralise the poison, and that is causing your pains and sickness and upsetting your body's chemical systems.	*Feels very cautious about being direct on the subject of 'alcohol' as talker fears this will break the tentative trust that has been established. To confront the denial may make him less receptive. But it is vital to keep to the task, as he will once again be denied the truth. Help him work through his defensiveness at his own pace.*
TOM	What – do you mean I'm eating something that does not agree with me?	*Feels scared. The greater the defence, the greater the fear beneath.*
DR P	No, not eating something – and I think at the back of your mind you might know what I'm talking about, although you probably don't really want to think about it.	*Perhaps the talker is also wary as scared of 'not getting it right' or, not knowing how to help, not providing the help that is 'expected'.*

TOM	What – are you suggesting I'M A BOOZER? I don't drink any more than my mates, and there are a lot of the lads who could drink me under the table. I used to drink a lot more before I got married. No doctor, really, it must be something else causing this stomach bother: I only have a few pints and I hardly ever get a hangover. What else could it be?	*Outburst of anger and anxiety suggests possibility of the truth. Feels scared. Drops defence of denial for a moment, to be replaced by rationalisation.*
DR P	Let's just say that the tests show without any doubt that your system is getting more alcohol into it than it can handle. Your friends might be drinking more, and they might not get stomach problems – but not many folk that regularly drink more than four or five pints a day can get away with it for very long.	*Keep to the task, to allow the message to sink in without accusative words. It may be tempting to feel protective of his anguish or irritated that he does not accept what talker is saying. The drinker's defences are too entrenched.*
TOM	What! Are you saying that I can't have more than a few pints?	*Feels frustrated and denied of what he feels he needs (see Chapter 3).*
DR P	All I'm saying at the moment is that the amount you are having is causing you harm. Now we need longer to talk about this and I've got to get on now. Will you read this booklet (*That's the Limit*) and fill in the chart on the back page about how much you drink each day, for a week and then come back and see me?	*Don't be swayed by the force of the defensive reaction by rejecting. Getting through the defences and helping the drinker through them is vital work. Help the drinker come to his own conclusions without the talker putting himself or being put in a position of authority to which the drinker can respond destructively.*
TOM	What about something for my stomach though?	*'I need help with my pain'.*

DR P	I think we both know what can make your stomach better. Medicines are not the answer when there is still so much poison in your system. Cut out the drink for a week we'll see how things are by next Friday. I think you're stomach may begin to feel a bit better. Remember to make an appointment before you go.	*Help him feel less alone with his struggle. It is easy for the talker to feel that he is not providing enough. Advice, support and encouragement provide a thread of support that the drinker may not have experienced in the past, and may enable him to face his problem in a different way.*

Dialogue (2) Interview with College Tutor and Student
Scene

The scene below describes a termly review of student (Ann) with her tutor. He is by nature ebullient and outspoken, and brings his personality to all relationships. Ann is in her first year, second term. She is not achieving; her academic performance has not lived up to her own or others' expectations. On starting the course, she was outgoing and it has been noted that she has been spending more time alone. It was thought that she was studying, but her work has not supported this. Her tutor is puzzled. It is 4pm and two weeks before the end of term.

TUTOR	God, what is the matter with you!	*Feels shocked at what he sees. Unable to hide this.*
ANN	*(Silence, sits with head in hands.)*	*Feels too withdrawn to speak.*
TUTOR	Last time we met you were full of life, enjoying yourself, going to parties.	*Continues his feedback. His ebullience increases in response to her silences.*
ANN	*(Silence, continues to look at the floor.)*	*Still feels withdrawn, but in spite of his outspokenness, feels accepted by him.*
TUTOR	*(Feels awkward, gets up and walks around the room.)*	
ANN	I want to jack it in.	*Feels she is able to speak as a result of his action. The intensity of the dialogue is reduced.*

Pause

TUTOR	*(quizzically)* Sorry?	*The severity of the situation is dawning. Needs to remain sensitive in response.*
ANN	I have had enough.	*Able to express the bare minimum. Feels too shut down to say more. Feeling very guilty, hopeless and despairing.*
TUTOR	You… you want to leave? But… but you are one of our best pupils. You were… signed up for fame and fortune… You had such a good…	*Ask the obvious as clearly things have gone very wrong. Trust the element of shock as it will help to find out what is really happening.*
ANN	Oh don't go on!	*Feels terrible pressure of failing expectations – not only her own, but other peoples'. Once again, feels she must defend herself from this pain, but becomes less withdrawn.*
TUTOR	*(moves around again)* I'm sorry, but I am a bit shocked. What on earth is going on!	*Responds to the need to release some tension. Needs time to think.*
ANN	*(lapses back into herself)* Oh! I don't know.	*Feels punished and interrogated and resorts to her initial position.*

A crucial stage in the dialogue has been reached. The tutor has an investment in his students staying on the course, and may feel some rejection and failure at the prospect of an academic student giving up. The student, meanwhile, is anticipating rejection and punishment for failure. Both the tutor and the student may well be feeling emotionally out of their depth. The student has decided to deal with this by leaving the course.

The tutor, however, still has some options. He has seen that by being shocked and outraged, he has silenced Ann again, most likely because she can anticipate a parental response of the same nature. She is withdrawn and depressed. He is outgoing by nature. It is vital he trusts his strengths and uses the undoubted assets of his personality to bridge the gap between their different worlds for the dialogue to continue.

After all, Ann has come to see him. She could have made an excuse.

TUTOR	OK (*firmly*) well, let me ask you this. You have the academic ability to do this course – I know that, but what I don't know is what has happened to you.	*Using his ebullience, but trying to reach her as a peer, not in judgment or in shock, or outrage.*
	Pause	
ANN	Oh I am not sure, I just don't feel like doing anything.	*Feeling a little stronger.*
TUTOR	You seem to have completely lost your spark.	*Don't rush her, she needs time.*
	Pause	
ANN	Things are just so different now.	*She is giving hints she would like someone to know more.*
TUTOR	How do you mean different? I can see that things have changed. You used to be so full of beans.	
ANN	Oh, I don't know.	*Feeling unsure again. Feels scared.*
TUTOR	I am not different, college is the same as ever. What's different?	*Keep encouraging her.*
	Pause	
ANN	It's just…	
TUTOR	Its just what? Come on, cough it up! Please tell me.	*Using his instincts. Ann will soon indicate if it is not helpful.*
	Pause	
TUTOR	Is it the work…?	
ANN	(*interrupting*) No, no. I never see anyone, I am not interested in going out. I just want to be at home.	*Feeling more moved to speak. Tutor beginning to feel more reassured.*
TUTOR	What would you do at home?	*It would be easy to give up with a situation like this and hope someone else might deal with it – a common response that drinkers face, as if it is too 'hot'. Ann needs*

help not to run away (see Chapter 4).

ANN I don't know, but it can't be worse than here.

TUTOR But look, Ann, you seem very down in the dumps to me.

ANN *(a little irritated)* I am! It is what this place has done to me. I hate it!

     Pause

Some anger may help her come out of herself a little.

TUTOR Well, what are we going to do about that then?

Keep to track.

ANN Leave, of course!

TUTOR Well, I think you are daft!

ANN You would! I have no option. It is a way out. I have not told a soul about this. You are the first person I have spoken to in days.

Responding to his directness. Giving more hints as to her distress. It is vital that these are picked up, as some trust is being developed between them.

TUTOR What are you doing with yourself? You can't just sit there all by yourself?

ANN I sit and stare at the walls, and think about the end of term.

Feels encouraged by his concern.

TUTOR Do you read? Watch telly? Go for a drink? What do you do with yourself?

There is no clear indication that Ann is drinking. Indeed, she may well be depressed. However, there is never any harm in asking. It can be a great relief to the drinker, and it is commonly the talker's avoidance or discomfort that makes it difficult to bring the subject up.

ANN Well, I try to escape, run away. I have the odd drink; maybe too much, really. It is all I have got. It helps me sleep, forget my troubles.

Feels able to entrust this information. A big step forward.

TUTOR So you are feeling down and booze helps.

Now she has entrusted the talker, it is important not to run away from the issue. She is beginning to acknowledge a problem. It is vital that the talker does too.

ANN Maybe more than it should. All because of this place. It makes me so miserable.

The pain of acknowledgement is reduced by putting the blame outside herself (see Chapter 3).

TUTOR Come on, it's not as simple as that. Are you telling me you're drinking because of this place and once you get home, everything will be all right?

The drinker will want the talker to buy this excuse. It is again vital that the talker does not collude. Again, use of instincts can be very valuable in this situation.

ANN But I hate it here.

Has to try and justify her statement.

TUTOR Sometimes I drink to make me feel better in myself.

Try and reach her so she does not have to feel defensive.

ANN It feels like a dream.

TUTOR Good dream or bad dream?

ANN A nightmare.

Another crucial stage of the interview, as Ann has now revealed the gravity of her problems. The tutor may well begin to feel out of his depth. His expertise is in tutoring and teaching, perhaps not in counselling. What is needed from him now is to realise and exercise his limitations and be clear to himself and to Ann what exactly he can offer. Ann has bestowed a huge amount of confidence in the talker – 'I have not spoken to anyone for days'. It is easy for the talker to get hoodwinked into thinking 'Therefore I am the only person who can help'. Unconsciously, Ann may be searching for something from her tutor that is inappropriate to the relationship. This may become unhelpful both for her recovery (see Chapters 3 and 4) and for the tutor, when the unfulfilled dependency needs and expectations from that relationship are not forthcoming. It is, therefore, important to recognise what is the most appropriate action to take at this point.

TUTOR	I don't want you to leave this course, because I think that would be a big waste. I am not prepared to let you go that easily.	
ANN	*(bursts into tears)* No I don't really want to go either.	
TUTOR	I can see you are in great distress. I think we need to help you get some help. I am your tutor. I am not in a position to help you myself, but I know there is Student Health Counselling where you can go for help.	
ANN	Mmm *(looks down)* I'm not sure. I'd have to think about it.	*Feels anxious and scared.*
TUTOR	Yes, but we could ring now... Now that we have got this far.	
ANN	I'm really not sure.	*Needs time to make this decision for herself.*
TUTOR	I realise you may feel rushed, but let's see what is involved and then we can make a decision as to the best way forward.	*Sensitive to being pushy, but he has gained her trust and confidence which she badly needs. Important to support her through indecision without taking away her initiative.*
ANN	OK, I'll see what's involved – but that's all!	

Ann remains understandably very cautious. It may take a long time for an individual to acknowledge the need for help. Supporting her during this time, with tolerance and patience, is invaluable work, although it is important to consider that the talker, in this case the tutor, may or may not see the fruits of that endeavour. For the talker to relinquish the need to see change may be the most valuable aspect of the work done and gives greatest freedom to the drinker.

CHAPTER 8

'Old Habits Die Hard' – Emerging Dependence

Dialogue (1) Conversation Between Health Visitor and Young Mother
Scene

A young mother (Joan) has recently been seen at the clinic for immunisation of her small boy (Thomas). She was seen by the staff to be on edge and restless, looking unhappy, but pushing away inquiries of concern. 'Oh I'm OK'. She has little immediate family support. Her husband is helpful but works long hours. By request from the clinic doctor, the Health Visitor (Sue) visits Joan at home.

SUE	Hello, how are things?	*Try and engage her trust.*
JOAN	Oh not too bad. Thomas is still not sleeping at night.	*Talker getting a feel of the scene.*
SUE	How often does he wake?	
JOAN	Two or three times a night.	
SUE	You must be getting tired.	
JOAN	And I can't sleep either. I thought of asking my doctor for some sleeping pills.	*Talker feeling some concern at the situation.*
SUE	Do you know why you are not sleeping?	*Start to clarify possibilities. Is she depressed?*
JOAN	Oh I don't know, I just feel restless.	
SUE	What do you do during the day?	

JOAN	I stay indoors. Perhaps pop out to the shop now and again. I seem to have so much work in the house, I can't catch up with myself.	
SUE	Do you not go and see people in the street?	*Sensing social isolation.*
JOAN	Well, sometimes. None of them have children, and Thomas is so active.	
SUE	He sounds a bit of a handful.	
JOAN	I just despair of him sometimes.	*Feels low.*
SUE	What about the local toddler group?	
JOAN	Well, I don't know anyone there ,and anyway, I have to be back to give Thomas his lunch.	*Low self-confidence, and increasingly rigid pattern of life.*
SUE	What about the evenings? Although I know that John gets back late.	
JOAN	Well, I can't go out anywhere, as Thomas is still up.	

A rather bleak picture of social isolation emerges. The talker may pick up that Joan is feeling helpless and trapped. When this arises in the conversation, maybe it is the time to inquire how she handles these feelings. The above describes an all too common scenario for a young mother and demanding child, and it is tempting to dispel any suspicions aroused about the possibility of drinking behaviour. But she has declared several problems that are disclosing her difficulties – sleeplessness in spite of being tired; lack of confidence and possibly some agoraphobia; agitated child; rigid regime that may fit into her drinking pattern. She may well be depressed. But it may well be the denial of the talker that eliminates the discussion of an emerging dependence on alcohol (see Chapter 4). It never does any harm to ask. If the talker is inhibited, so is the drinker. Raising the issue of alcohol can feel scary, but it can also create relief.

SUE   You sound rather unhappy.

JOAN   That's nothing new.

SUE   Do have any ways of cheering
        yourself up?

JOAN   No, not really. Going out at
        weekends sometimes.

SUE   You're a smoker aren't you?

JOAN   Yes, couldn't do without those.

SUE   Ever have a drink?

JOAN   Perhaps one or two while I'm
        cooking the tea, It helps to keep
        me going.

A crucial point of the interview has been reached. Joan has declared a plausible position. The talker has to make an overall assessment of Joan's situation. Alcohol may or may not be contributing. Trust has been gained and there may be a fear that confrontation will betray that trust (see Chapter 4). The fear may lie with the talker. There is nothing to lose by asking.

SUE   Is it just one or two?

JOAN   That depends on how I am
        feeling.

SUE   What do you drink?   *Search for some clarification of*
                                          dependence.

JOAN   Wine or sherry.

SUE   Do you ever worry that you   *Important to assess the response to*
        drink too much?   *a question like this as it can clarify*
                                          how the drinker perceives her
                                          drinking.

An important stage of the dialogue has been reached as the subject of alcohol has been broached. Below, several scenes are described to illustrate the wide range of possible responses that the talker has to listen for after an inquiry about drinking.

Scene 1. Clarifying the picture

JOAN   Well, that is all I have. Otherwise   *Acknowledgement of psychological*
         I would never get to sleep.   *dependency.*

SUE   Does your husband know that   *Find how much she has been able*
         you feel this way?   *to communicate her distress.*

JOAN   No, I don't want him to know
         about it. I feel too ashamed.

To help assess a more comprehensive picture of dependence, the talker can use the CAGE four item screening test (see Chapter 4) in the knowledge that alcohol increases anxiety and sleeplessness and lowers self-esteem (see Chapter 1).

SUE   Have you ever felt you needed
         to cut down your drinking?

JOAN   I have tried but I don't see the
         point.

SUE   Have you felt annoyed that
         others criticise your drinking?

JOAN   Nobody knows what I do
         indoors.

SUE   Have you ever felt guilty about
         what you drink?

JOAN   Well, *(looking down)* we don't   *Can acknowledge some guilt.*
         have much money.

SUE   I appreciate that, but that does
         not deter some people from
         having a drink first thing in the
         morning. Do you ever do that?

JOAN   *(remains looking at the floor and
         mumbles)* I've thought about it.

SUE	Alcohol, strange as it may seem, makes you more restless, can disrupt your sleep and make you feel more down in the dumps. Why don't you try not drinking for a few days and see how you feel?	*The response to this suggestion may clarify the extent of dependency still further by the amount of resistance to this idea.*
JOAN	But how can I? What else can I do?	*Feels very scared. A picture of psychological dependence emerging.*
SUE	I appreciate it may feel very difficult to think about stopping drinking. It takes great courage. But nor is it making you happy. If anything, I think it is making you feel worse.	*Be supportive but realistic.*
JOAN	I feel ghastly.	
SUE	I suggest you have no drink in the house so there is no temptation. And every time you feel like a drink, do something with Thomas. He would certainly like that.	*The talker needs to remember that a picture of physical dependence may emerge if she does stop drinking.*
SUE	If you feel strange in the next few days, you must contact your GP or me. It may be the effects of stopping drinking. Don't struggle with it alone. I will come and see you tomorrow after lunch, about 2pm, and we can see how things are then. In the mean time, if you are in trouble, just ring me.	*Make definite appointment so that the drinker has something secure and tangible to hold onto. The next few days will feel scary and uncertain.* *(See Chapters 3 and 4).*

Having considered that Joan may have an alcohol problem, the talker needs to take stock as to the next step, and to be helpful in the subsequent stages. The talker may leave this interview with some questions:

- Have I done enough?
- Have I said the right thing?
- Will I make her drinking worse?

- Perhaps I have got it all wrong?
- Will she be all right?

There will be no Yes or No answers to these questions (see Chapters 4 and 5). The talker has to consider whose anxieties and responsibilities she is carrying and whether they are her own or those of the drinker. The responsibility of the talker at this stage is to:

1. maintain support

2. keep looking clearly for signs of distress

3. acquaint oneself with services and facilities that are appropriate for advice and help, for example AA, local counselling services, drop in centres, mothers' support groups

4. discuss with colleague any doubts or concerns

5. in preparation for next visit, get leaflets and phone numbers.

From the CAGE assessment, where two or more positives would suggest a heavy drinking problem, the talker in this dialogue would have a clear indication that Joan is most likely concealing an alcohol problem. This may create huge distress and embarrassment for Joan; a sense of relief and reduced isolation may be experienced just as keenly.

It is important to bear in mind that, even if the situation seems greatly different at the next visit, dependency on alcohol is a long term problem and she may have to face similar conflicts many times in the future. Drinkers are apt to defend their real needs and may not be able to pinpoint them for themselves. Even if the talker's suggestions are not accepted, it is the responsibility of the talker to stay to the task of giving information.

Possible Scenario

SUE   Hello, how are you?

JOAN   Oh I am much better now. I haven't had a drink since I last saw you.

SUE   I am glad about that. You look a lot brighter. I have brought you some information about a local drop-in centre where you can go for a coffee and a chat. It is quite close to here. I have also brought some leaflets about Alcoholics Anonymous.

Whatever the answer, give the appropriate information. She may be on the road to recovery or she may have shut the door harder. The talker will not always know.

JOAN   But I am all right now. I don't need those! And anyway, I am not an alcoholic.

SUE   I agree that you seem brighter and happier. But from what we talked about last time we met, you seem to be vulnerable to drinking a bit too much when things are getting you down. I think that it is very important that you bear that in mind, and begin to recognise this for yourself. AA is there for all those who struggle to control their drinking in difficult times, and they will be the first to tell you that it is nothing to be ashamed of. It is also quite a good idea to make contact when you are feeling good, just in case things go downhill a bit. Everyone there is very friendly.

Be clear but firm. Important not to get swept along in her buoyancy.

JOAN   But I won't know anybody.

SUE   I know, but in this leaflet there are telephone numbers of those who will come and see you at home, and they will take you along if you like.

Pause

I will leave these leaflets with you so that you can look at them in your own time. How's Thomas? (*The interview may now turn to other concerns for both parties*).

The talker needs to keep visiting and maintaining trust. Continue to ask about alcohol and her response to your suggestions. Be mindful of relapse (see Chapter 10) and don't let the door close again.

Scene 2. Working with Denial

Returning to the initial inquiry by the talker concerning drinking, the response may be somewhat different.

SUE	Do you ever worry that you drink too much?	
JOAN	No. I feel better for it and it helps to pass the time.	*Unable to be clear if there is a problem but does portray a sense of feeling very alone.*

Joan may have no problems with alcohol and may be drinking in an appropriate way. Or the talker may find that Joan is not able to be honest with herself or the talker about the extent of her drinking, and continues to disguise her drinking. This may become evident quickly or the denial may be protracted for a considerable time. The talker needs to remain open minded to this possibility. Commonly, this can evoke a feeling of resentment, frustration, professional helplessness and being undermined. It is equally common for the client to be 'blamed' for lack of co-operation, being devious, unhelpful and so on.

It is almost certain that the client will be feeling the same as the talker, with greater intensity, either with herself or those around her (see Chapter 4). What is common to both talker and drinker is that this is a crucial point in the relationship. 'Holding' the denial is vital work on behalf of the talker. If the talker turns away, the drinker will once again experience that her problems cannot be faced or contained, adding to an already strong sense of rejection.

So too, the talker may well face aspects of herself that require client co-operation and compliance. Both parties need to keep their dialogues open. The talker needs to explore her own issues with colleagues. The drinker needs to be able to continue to talk to the talker at her own pace, without the fear of feeling punished or rejected. Coming to see that there is a problem is vital work.

Possible Scenario. Perhaps two or three weeks later.

SUE	Hello, how are you?	
JOAN	Oh, I'm OK.	
SUE	Just OK?	
JOAN	Well, nothing has changed really.	*Feels a bit hopeless.*
SUE	You mentioned before that you hadn't been sleeping very well.	*The task is to reflect back to what the drinker has said without being too confrontative and to make it clear that you can tolerate and*

		acknowledge that things are not all *'OK'.*
JOAN	Thomas is still waking so much.	*Having difficulty acknowledging her own distress.*
SUE	He seems a rather restless little chap. Do you think you are alike?	*Help her to open up and make it easy for you both to talk.*
JOAN	I was just the same when I was small. I was shut in my bedroom because my Mum said she couldn't cope with me. I used to hate her when she did that.	
SUE	That must have been horrid. Why do you think she did that?	*Help her to keep talking and listen carefully to the information.*
JOAN	I don't know. She was so erratic. Sometimes I could sit downstairs. Other times I was bundled off upstairs. *Pause* I suppose I am a bit like that with Thomas, when I have had a bad day.	
SUE	Do you think your Mum had 'bad days'?	
JOAN	Usually when she had had the sherry bottle out.	
SUE	Is that the same for you?	*This question may be getting 'hot', but indicates that the talker is continuing to address the issue. Don't be pushed off track. Her mother was inconsistent. It is important that the talker is consistent and reliable. Help Joan reflect.*
JOAN	I don't know, I had never thought about it.	

SUE	Perhaps it is worth thinking about this. We all do different things for different reasons, and it is sometimes helpful to consider the whys and wherefores. I think it is hard to talk about oneself, but I hope we can continue to do this over time. How's Thomas?

This dialogue could take many forms, but serves to illustrate how to help the drinker begin to reflect, open some doors without being too intrusive. Clearly this demands time, commitment and trust and aims to enable greater self-disclosure, ultimately working through the drinker's own denial, to acknowledge whatever degree of alcohol dependency is present. Indeed, this very process may well enable the drinker to relinquish her dependence on alcohol. The dependence can, in some cases, become transferred onto the talker, a phenomenon often feared by workers in the field and commonly avoided by premature termination of a therapeutic relationship, or conversely, a reluctance to get 'too involved' (see Chapter 4 and Chapter 5).

Alternatively, a clear picture of physical dependency may emerge.

Scene 3. Acting on disclosure

SUE	Hello, how are you today?	
JOAN	Oh, I'm OK	
SUE	Just OK?	
JOAN	Well, I'm feeling a bit restless and a bit churned up.	*Signs of physical dependence present.*
SUE	OK. That must be very unpleasant. Have you told anybody else about this?	*Acknowledge her distress. Clarify who she has been able to communicate with.*
JOAN	No, I can't even go out.	*Fear and embarrassment.*
SUE	When did you last have a drink?	*Important as this will suggest the level of dependence and how far through the process of withdrawal she may be (see Chapter 1).*

JOAN	I finished the bottle yesterday.	*From this answer, Joan will be going into a withdrawal state as her blood/alcohol level will be dropping. Talker may need to consider seeking some medical consultation. Glean further symptoms.*
SUE	Are you eating anything?	
JOAN	I just feel too sick.	
SUE	Do you feel very shaky?	
JOAN	Inside I do. I can't sit still for a minute.	
SUE	Would you be prepared to go and see your doctor?	
JOAN	No! I can't do that.	*Feels embarrassed, vulnerable and exposed. Needs lots of support and important to act before resumption of drinking or return of denial.*
SUE	Shall I come with you?	
JOAN	John will be home soon and he will be wondering what is happening.	*Trying desperately to keep her life together.*
SUE	Have you told him anything?	
JOAN	No (*looks crestfallen*).	*Very difficult time as everything will be happening at once. Help the drinker not to backtrack.*
JOAN	But why should I go to the doctor? I am all right really.	
SUE	There can be some risks to your health when you stop drinking. I would just like him to know how you are and what is happening for you. He may decide to give you something to	

make you feel a bit calmer, for
the time being.

JOAN   Will he give me something to   *Suggests how desperate she feels.*
       help me sleep?

SUE   That would be for him to decide.   *Be clear with the facts with out*
       I think you will find that it is the *giving false promises. They can*
       alcohol that has made you so   *trip the drinker up at a later stage.*
       restless and sleepless.

JOAN   But John is coming home soon,   *Some practical issues to address,*
       as I say. And what about   *but maybe disguising fear and*
       Thomas?   *some reluctance to come forward.*

SUE   How soon will he be back?   *Help her directly with these issues.*

JOAN   At about 4.00pm.

SUE   Why don't I come round about   *Remain available for discussion*
       4.30 and help you to explain the   *and decision making, but enable*
       situation to John, and from   *the drinker to retain some power,*
       there, we will make an   *control and responsibility*
       appointment to see your GP. You   *However, the talker has to keep in*
       might like John to go with you.   *mind the priority of helping the*
       These are the things we need to   *drinker before she changes her*
       discuss.   *mind.*

JOAN   OK, but I might change my   *As feared, this comment can open*
       mind.   *the whole discussion again. It may*
                                           increase a defensive reaction on
                                           behalf of the drinker. State
                                           commitment of intent. That is the
                                           most important thing to do.

SUE   I will see you at 4.30.

This dialogue illustrates perhaps only the start of the journey for a hitherto
'undisclosed' drinker, albeit an important step for both drinker and talker. Sue
will have to decide on her role within the context of Joan's drinking problem.
Liaison with other parties who will become involved is crucial.

Dialogue (2) Changing Jobs to Accommodate Drinking

Scene

A factory worker (John) comes to discuss a transfer from day shift to night shift. At face value, this seems a reasonable request. He has been with the firm some time and, until recently, his work record has been good. He is putting his request to his line manager (Bill). Bill has become increasing concerned about John's erratic attendance and has suspected but has had no evidence that drink has become a problem. John is often seen in the pub.

The talker's task is not merely to listen to the request and respond, but to try and help John explore the motives behind his wish to move. His past experience tells him that simply agreeing to the request could be colluding with the drinker and result in the deterioration of the situation by making it easier for consumption to increase.

BILL   Hello, come and sit down.

JOHN	I'd... er... like to... er transfer to night shift.	*Feels anxious. Unsure as to how he will be received.*

The opening statements of this conversation brings the dialogue quickly to a potentially difficult point. Bill, the line manager may have accumulated considerable frustration with John's recent poor work performance and he may well see this as an opportunity to discuss these things, particularly as John is asking for something (see Chapters 4 and 5). Making sure the work is efficiently tackled and completed is clearly his job. There is a fine line between the use and abuse of power. The 'abuse' of power is something the drinker may have previously experienced and may exacerbate his drinking and therefore his erratic behaviour.

John, feeling guilty and 'knowing' his recent poor performance, feels desperate and is asking for help in a heavily disguised form. But he may be anticipating the worst, because of his guilt. Perhaps the talker's task, here, is to confront his recent poor performance, to explore why he wants a different shift and point out that his behaviour needs to change in order to get what he wants. Instant collusion with his request, tempting though this might be, will help nothing and will deepen his problem, passing it on elsewhere. It is as easy for the talker as the drinker 'to avoid' the problem.

BILL   Oh, I see. Why is that? When you first joined us you wouldn't work on nights for love nor money. What's changed?

JOHN	I don't get enough money on days. My wife is always complaining I don't give her enough.	*The drinker can no longer meet the cost of his drinking. His compulsion to drink drives him into stressful situations, for example this interview. He is denying his anxiety and displaces the responsibility onto his wife.*
BILL	Your wife used to have a job. Is she not working now?	*Pick up the theme that things may have changed. Create some trust to see if he is prepared to be more open about his position.*
JOHN	Oh yes, but that doesn't bring in very much.	*Can't risk picking up any openings, as not wishing to face things himself.*
BILL	I realise you don't earn a fortune on days, but you always used to manage. I am still wondering what has changed and if nights will really help.	*Be straight about the obvious inconsistencies, as the drinker is too defensive and frightened to explore them himself. The talker is having to balance between gaining trust and confrontation.*
JOHN	Well, I think it would.	*Feels irritated that he needs to explain himself.*
BILL	I AM concerned that you don't get enough money. But my primary concern is that your attendance has been somewhat erratic of late: you seem dreamy and preoccupied, not getting on with the job in hand; the other lads are fed up with covering up...	*Talker feels a little impatient in response. Important to air some truths without being too punitive.*
JOHN	*(interrupts)* I keep oversleeping.	*Feels very scared and therefore more defensive.*

Silence

	It's the children. They keep me awake half the night.	*Struggling to find excuses.*

BILL — Come on, John, I wasn't born yesterday. I realise it may be tough at home but that doesn't cause people to take days off. I think there is more behind this request than meets the eye.

Don't be drawn into his excuses, or be too punitive. The drinker is frightened.

JOHN — Well, as far as I am concerned I just want more money.

Unable to see his enormous rationalisation, and unable to face up to the exploration.

BILL — As far as I am concerned, things will have to improve here first, as I am in no position to recommend you to another shift. Perhaps we need to think of ways of first making that improvement.

Again, the talker may be swayed by the plausible rationalisation. Be clear about personal experience and perception of the drinker, and extend some offer of help and hope.

JOHN — I am only asking to work on night shift. I am fed up with this shift.

Feels too scared to respond to invitation and feels pretty fed up that he is not getting what he wants straight away.

BILL — I think we both know that night shift is no different to this shift. In fact, it can be even worse.

Reflect back his own rationalisation. He may be ready 'to run', so there is a need to be cautious.

Pause

In my experience, there are usually reasons why people oversleep, and my advice to you is to think carefully about why you are late for work and missing days. I am aware that you may not want to discuss things further with me, but there are others to talk to, who might be able to help sort things out and I would be happy to help you think of the right person. It may be here, it could be elsewhere. I hear your request, but there are several issues to tackle first. Let me know what you decide.

The door remains open for both parties to continue the dialogue.

The Citizens Advice Bureau may give advice with problems of debt.

It may seem more attractive but may prove less helpful in the longer term.

The root of the problem, alcohol, has not been mentioned. It seems too early and not the right setting to open that particular door. However, the 'drinking thinking' has been addressed and the talker has not been swept into its wake. The talker has been clear about where he stands, and has left an opening for John to instigate change. This may be a long and at times painful process for talker and drinker alike. Often, the talker wants to be able to help and even 'do it all'. That responsibility has to be left to the drinker, with clear guidance as to where and how advice can be sought (see Chapter 4).

CHAPTER 9

'Problems Galore' – A Multitude of Things Start Going Wrong

Dialogue (1) Family break-up. Consultation at a Voluntary Agency

Scene

Keith has referred himself to a voluntary agency that is staffed with trained counsellors dealing with alcohol and substance misuse. He is a self employed electrician and is married to Jane. They are both in their early fifties, and have three children from their twenty five year marriage.

Keith has had one consultation at the agency. The counsellor (Pam) invites him to bring Jane along as some of the difficulties he is describing seem to have roots in their marital relationship and Keith is asking Pam to help his wife. To help Jane become involved, Pam has to acknowledge that her relationship with Keith will have to change. Jane has agreed to come but is quite indignant and somewhat fearful.

Conversation in waiting room

JANE	Well, fancy ending up in a place like this!	*Feels a great mixture of things – anger, despair, resignation.*
KEITH	We need help. We can't go on, you need...	*Feels equally desperate, but more optimistic.*
PAM	Hello, I'm Pam.	
JANE	Yes, and I'm Jane. I've heard about you from Keith.	
KEITH	Hello.	
PAM	Shall we go along to a more comfortable room?	

Once seated...

PAM	It is good to see you both and to meet you, Jane. I overheard a bit of your conversation just now. I am wondering what it is that makes you feel you need help?	*Important to make Jane feel included. Remain mindful of their already declared 'neediness'.*
JANE	I think Keith is the one in need. He's the one who hasn't been able to cope recently. I don't think I need anything.	
KEITH	That's not how I see it. I came here because of you and your drinking.	*Both defending themselves from their own difficulties by seeing themselves in the other partner, a common defence against emotional pain (see Chapters 3 and 4). This allows room for denial.*
JANE	I'm all right. You keep telling me I have a problem. It's not a problem to me, Keith. So what's the matter with you?	*Denial is often recognised by rather accusatory and hostile statements.*
PAM	It sounds as though you both have a problem. It may or may not be the same one, but could we start by each of you having the chance to say why you are here. Jane – why do you think you are here?	*Important to remain objective towards both parties. Begin to dislodge the mutually held misperceptions by clarifying their differences and also the similarities on which their relationship is based.*
JANE	Because he says I drink too much.	*Unable to clarify her real needs and puts the responsibility onto Keith. Feels punished by him.*
PAM	Anything else?	
JANE	And I want to know what he has been saying about me.	*Loss of trust? Fears of misrepresentation, 'blackened character', biased information.*
PAM	And Keith?	
KEITH	You know, we've been through it before.	*Would like to maintain the special relationship from which he has*

		drawn some comfort. This will also exclude Jane as drink excludes him.
PAM	It is important that Jane hears from you why you are here.	*Very easy to side with Keith, thus mirroring their marriage. Convey impartiality. Is this marriage is already cluttered with misalliances (see Chapter 2)?*
KEITH	She drinks too much. She had one today before coming here. I need to tell you the truth.	*Wants to be seen as the 'good' guy. Perhaps there is a desire to perpetuate the myth that Jane is 'the problem' (see Chapter 2).*
JANE	Why, that's not true, and you know it.	*Feels scared of 'the truth'.*
PAM	Why do you think Keith would wish to say something if it were not the truth?	*Be careful with wording in order to maintain neutrality. There are risks of being asked and seen to be taking sides.*
JANE	He just wants to put me in a bad light. He is no angel but I don't suppose he has told you what he does. He's off all day, leaves me with all the housework and the children to worry about. He's often home late – been with his mates in the pub.	*No trust. Anger and resentment. Suggestion of her own unmet dependency needs. Strong sense of not being valued.*
KEITH	Yes, but why? It's awful at home. One of the kids is truanting, another doesn't speak, and you're drunk.	*He cannot cope with his own feelings of failure and guilt, and so 'puts' them at Jane's door.*

This is an interesting example of how differently individuals manifest their dependency needs and how they are met in a mutual relationship. Jane is resentful and secretive; Keith is evasive and searching for help. This is commonly found in a 'drinking' partnership (see Chapters 3 and 4).

However, it is the drinking that is the most easily identifiable 'symptom' of mutual dependency and is therefore seen as the 'problem' (see systems theory, Chapter 2).

PAM	Besides Keith's worries, why are you here?	*Continue to explore their differences.*

JANE	Well, he says he is off if something doesn't happen.	*Feels scared and threatened.*
KEITH	I've had enough! She drinks every day, she isn't reliable, she...	
PAM	Keith, Jane is sitting there. Can you speak to her?	*Help build some bridges.*
KEITH	I try, how I try, but she never listens. You've seen it just now. She has had a drink. She's forgotten, so she argues or says I am telling lies.	*Entrenched position that he wants confirmed. It feels easier to talk about Jane than to her.*
PAM	I know it is difficult to talk openly about what is going on, but it is necessary that you both start to talk to each other. Can you try again?	*Important that the isolation is reduced, and that there is an attempt to shift the entrenchment.*
KEITH	You drink too much! I'm fed up and I will go if it doesn't get better.	*Feels desperate and out of control.*
JANE	You have said that before, but you don't, do you?	*Recognition of his dependency on her.*
KEITH	I really don't want to. But it is getting too much.	*Perhaps recognises the same thing.*
PAM	What do you think Keith means?	
JANE	I'm not sure but I don't iron his shirts like I used to. We never go anywhere together anymore – I get tired. It's all right for him, he comes and goes as he pleases, never stops to think how boring it can be at home all day, apart from a couple of hours at school.	*Loss of self and self esteem. Envious of his freedom and angry about his neglect, that she has allowed to happen.*

KEITH	Get tired! Huh! It is because you're too drunk to do anything. It is just an excuse to do nothing. You don't think of anyone but yourself. You don't look after the kids any more.	*His needs not being met. He is describing considerable loss – a loss of Jane to alcohol and a loss of the past.*
KEITH	Look at you! (*to Pam*) She used to be a really smart capable woman, with lots of interests and friends and it's all gone. I'd like it to be like that again.	*He is also rather envious that her needs are being met through alcohol.*
JANE	When it was like that, you didn't like it because I needed your help to do things in the house. We did a lot of rowing, as I remember it.	*Describing a different balance of interaction (system).*
PAM	When did things change?	
KEITH	Jane was a shop assistant, in a good dress shop in town. Then, with me going self-employed and with the children to organise, it didn't really fit in with family life. So she looked for something else. She missed her friends, time away from the house and the money, but the job at the school was very convenient. We always talked of her going back but she never did. She could, now the children are older. But it's too late now.	*Keith's move to 'independence', being self-employed, placed a different burden on Jane and she responded to this by drinking.*
PAM	Was that how you saw it, Jane? It sounds as if you made some big sacrifices for your family.	*Find out what Jane's perspective is. Important to acknowledge Jane's contribution towards change, otherwise she can again be seen as the victim.*
JANE	I didn't mind stopping work, but why has it all gone wrong?	*'Why am I carrying all the responsibility/dependency?'*

PAM	Perhaps you have both lost sight of what you have in common. It sounds to me as if you both want to do things in your own way, and you get cross with each other when you get in each other's way. You both need to have a chance to look at each other as individuals and share that, rather than resent each other for it. I think you both need some time to think about how things could be different.	*Begin to clarify the fact that they have mutual feelings of envy and dependence that they deal with badly, and paradoxically have in common. Remember their opening statements of need.*
JANE	I hate all this talk of change, all this suggestion that I am a drunk. I want someone to listen to me, to hear my side of the story.	*'I want to be seen as an individual and not as a dependant.'*
PAM	Yes, that sounds very important for you, Jane, as this is perhaps what you experience in your marriage. I am sure it would be possible for you to see one of my colleagues.	*Important to recognise that both have needs and Jane has not been 'heard' for some considerable time. Also important that neither is identified as 'the patient'.*

It is important for the talker to recognise that seeing a couple together if one partner is drinking may seem very punishing for the drinker. The partner who is not drinking may feel the need to 'report' on drinking behaviour in the session in order to represent his case.

KEITH	But what about me?	*Feels he needs help.*
PAM	I can offer to see you twice more, whilst Jane is being seen. I suggest that we then all come together, review things and see what help you would like. You may wish to pursue things together, or separately, or indeed not at all.	
KEITH	But I want to know if Jane is going to stop drinking.	*Keith is expressing his great anxiety about any potential change.*

Pam	I think that is for Jane and her counsellor to discuss and you can talk to me about your worries on that score. Jane, I will introduce you to Sally. Keith, I can make you an appointment for next week.	*Important to retain neutrality at this point.*

Jane has not declared that she has an alcohol problem. Keith has, on her behalf. She therefore needs time to come to her own conclusion about this and decide whether she does in fact want to pursue further help.

It is also important to recognise what resources and expertise are available in any one agency or setting. It is tempting to respond to the needs of others, before assessing personal and professional limitations – but this may result in a feeling of being overburdened with the strain. Can Pam take on a couple for intensive marital work? She would need to think about this carefully. Discussion with colleagues is valuable. One recognised way of doing this is to take some time out of the interview for discussion. This prevents the talker from being too overwhelmed with the presenting needs of the interview and gives time to make an informed, carefully thought out decision (Burnham 1988).

Every helping agency may have (and perhaps needs) a policy to follow, which can make decisions of this nature easier. And there are other resources to draw on such as RELATE (marriage guidance), Al-Anon, and perhaps Alcoholics Anonymous if and when Jane wants to go.

Dialogue (2) Helping the Potentially Aggressive

Scene

Mr Jocelyn is a man aged 35 who presents in the casualty department of a district general hospital, saying that he has a badly swollen ankle. He is sweating and anxious. After waiting 20 minutes he demands to be seen quickly. The sister on duty notices that his breath smells of alcohol and remembers seeing him on previous occasions.

Just before the nurse enters the cubicle, Mr Jocelyn overhears a conversation between staff:

Sister	*(to nurse)* – Will you go and talk with the man in cubicle 5? He smells strongly of alcohol. It's a little early for him to be drunk – but we have seen him before and he had been drinking on that occasion as well.	*Sister is anxious and transmitting some of her worry to her colleague. This, in turn, may alert her to the possibility of a difficult interview.*

Many factors need to be considered in this dialogue, even before the talker 'meets' the drinker. Prior knowledge about an individual may help the talker prepare for a clear assessment. That knowledge may also arouse prejudice and may cloud professional judgment. Such 'prejudice' is not uncommon when talking to those who meet drinkers in their work. Fear, dread and resentment may indicate a difficulty for the talker to offer help (see Chapters 4 and 5), and needs to be recognised rather than ignored, denied or swept under the carpet. It is not unprofessional to share one's fears with colleagues. Honesty is what we are asking for from the drinker. The drinker may be expecting certain responses from the 'professionals' and be looking for perceived repetition of past experiences – rejection, hostility, resentment (see Chapter 3). An insensitive response can only serve him ill by reinforcing his expectations.

In the light of this important issue, some time may be needed, if at all possible, to consider who is the 'best' person to help this gentleman. It can happen that those with most expertise can delegate to those with least experience as an unconscious avoidance of those whom they feel least able to help (see Chapter 5). This may reduce the potential therapeutic value of the time spent with the drinker, once again affirming his expectations and, perhaps in the long term, creating more stress and work. Communication between 'professionals' needs to be clear and open, away from the drinker, recognising personal anxieties and concerns. Decisions need to be made on the basis of this discussion (see Chapter 5).

Mr J.	I just want to make one thing clear – I'm not drunk, I'm in pain – and I want something done about it.	*The pain is not only physical; he is seeking help by repeating a pattern of adopting a defensive position to hide his problem. This has been heightened by the overheard comments. He feels very vulnerable, shouting in order to be heard.*
Nurse	I would like to help but I need to know what's been happening to you and why you've come to us today.	*Be calm. The drinker feels very chaotic. Be cautious about making promises. They make the talker feel better.*
Mr J.	I'm in pain. Will you get a doctor quickly, if you are not able to do anything yourself?	*Wants to get control of situation if not of himself. Needs reassurance but compensates by questioning her competence and authority (see Chapter 3).*
Nurse	Where is your pain and how long have you had it?	*Respond to his overt need. Talker establishes the boundaries of the*

		interview and is not ruffled by his emotional torrent and demands. Avoids taking up his challenge and continues to gather relevant information.
MR J.	It's my ankle. It's agony.	*Responds to limits and answers appropriately. Feels calmer as feels he is being heard.*
NURSE	What happened? It looks very swollen to me.	*Keep to task.*
MR J.	I fell over, tripped over the bloody pavement as I got out of my car. I was already late to see my client. I do wish they kept the streets in better condition. This is such a waste of time having to come here. I hope you can sort me out quickly as I have another client waiting.	*Feels irritated, frustrated, externalising blame. Scared of 'stopping'.*

A picture emerges of a rather frantic man, whose pattern of life has been temporarily interrupted by a physical injury, which is preventing him from continuing to 'run', both physically and psychologically. He is defensive, frightened and trying to cope by taking charge. It would be tempting for the nurse just to 'patch up' his ankle. However, he has clearly been drinking and has disclosed that he has recently been driving, quite possibly to get himself to the hospital. He is almost certainly over the legal limit and this begs the moral question as to how best to manage such a situation.

Mr Jocelyn is inadvertently presenting a chaotic, drinking lifestyle. Interception of such a way of life often occurs only when there has been an 'accident', preventing intense activity from continuing. Therapeutic intervention at that moment may be deeply resented at first but, in the longer term, greatly appreciated. It takes courage from both parties and can be 'lifesaving', especially when driving is involved.

NURSE	You seem in a dreadful rush. Sit down and let's talk about what has been happening for you.	*Talker needs to calm him down, not get engulfed in drinker's need and reflect back what is. Communicate concern for his distress to help establish some therapeutic alliance.*

MR J.   Look, I've just told you. I tripped over the pavement, hurt my ankle and want someone to look at it.

Feels frightened and trapped. Responds with hostility.

NURSE   Yes, I can see it looks very swollen. It is not usual for a fit man like yourself to trip and fall. This concerns me.

Helps him to feel heard and communicates the incongruity of his presentation.

MR J.   It is not usual for nurses to ask impertinent questions.

'Keep off, I am too scared to be confronted'.

NURSE   It is our job to find out about the whole picture.

Very hard to keep to task after such an apparently cutting remark. But there is a need to consider the whole picture. It may help to extend to the 'team' for momentary support away from personalisation.

MR J.   OK, I fell because I was in a hurry and got distracted by a passer-by that I thought I recognised.

Helped by talker's clarity and feels less defensive.

NURSE   And, as the ward sister noticed, there is a strong smell of alcohol in here.

Courageous but necessary. Creative use of the 'team' approach. This is not an accusation, it is an observation. Important to gauge his response.

MR J.   It is not against the law to drink. I have just had a meeting with a client and I am on my way to see another unless you keep me here indefinitely, answering these damn fool questions. When is something going to be DONE?

Fear intensifies and hostility and rationalisation return to push her away. Yearns for the immediate relief that alcohol can provide.

At this stage, the talker may feel bullied, punished and undermined by the drinker's response and may, too, feel like 'running away' or alternatively, counter attacking (see Chapters 4 and 5). Both would 'break' the fragile relationship that is present. Successful intervention may be brought about by treading cautiously but clearly:

NURSE	I think there are important medical considerations here which need further discussing. I will need you to see the doctor. Would you wait here and I'll tell him you are waiting?	*The drinker is scared. Important not to be patronising or to give the sense that the talker is 'running' for help. That will increase the drinker's fear.*
MR J.	(*shouting*) – Tell him I can't wait long!	

The nurse leaves the cubicle and, on her return, Mr Jocelyn has gone. A little time later a porter tells her that the man she was talking to earlier is lying in the gents lavatory, quite drunk and abusive. He asks the nurse whether he should arrange to have him removed by the security staff. The nurse declines, but enlists the help of a male colleague to go with her to talk to Mr Jocelyn in the lavatory. (Important to ensure safe practice, see Chapter 5).

NURSE	Mr Jocelyn, do you think you can get up so we can see if there is any way to help you?

It is very important that the nurse has returned to see Mr Jocelyn, and not had him 'removed'. This is what he was setting himself up for. The talker has not contributed to that cycle of self-destruction. However, it is also important that the nurse gets help, so that she feels adequately supported, particularly in the unfamiliar environment to which Mr Jocelyn has taken himself. Perhaps it is significant that he has taken himself to the one place where he cannot be reached by the very person who has offered help. Likewise, the nurse is right to continue the dialogue and rapport that has already been established, rather than asking the male colleague to do this. An unfamiliar, dominating force can feel very threatening and can readily lead, through fear, to unwanted provocation.

MR J.	I told you I couldn't wait long... I may as well go if the only thing that I can get here is a lecture on the evils of drinking.	*...for a drink. Perhaps he is communicating the extent of his alcohol dependency.*
NURSE	I want you to see the doctor. Your ankle is in poor shape.	*Be directive and firm.*
MR J.	Well, he can f... well wait, like I have had to. I'm off.	*Feels humiliated, insignificant, yet trapped by the position he has taken.*

| NURSE | He is waiting now. | *Be clear. Give the drinker a chance to turn around without having to lose face.* |
| MR J. | Too bad, let him stew. I'm going. | *Feels too scared to face this situation.* |

This is a difficult moment for the nurse as it may feel like a relief for Mr Jocelyn to leave. However, there have been suggestions that he is likely to drive; he may even have his car on the premises. In reality, in hard pressed casualty wards, Mr Jocelyn would leave without challenge. This scenario raises the moral issues of whether or not to allow an individual to drive when intoxicated and turn a blind eye, or whether to try and make an intervention. The same scene can emerge with friends and relatives. In the case of Mr Jocelyn, his drinking will undoubtedly 'catch up' with him. It begs the question of how much damage he might do to himself and/or others before he is 'caught' and to whom that difficult task will fall. The nurse in this scene could grasp hold of this but it takes great courage. There may be and indeed, perhaps there should be policy guidelines as to how to tackle the task. With a witness present, below is a possible illustrative approach:

NURSE	You are, of course, free to go. It is your choice whether you leave these premises but I am very concerned that you are going to drive and I feel you are probably well over the legal limit.	*Once again a potential point of confrontation. Again talker needs to be clear in her message without being too punishing.*
MR J.	It is none of your business what I do.	
NURSE	I am afraid it is my business. You can wait and see the doctor and sober up, or I can ring for a taxi to take you home.	*Be clear of your options and help him to see them too.*
Mr J.	(*walking towards the door*) – I will look after myself, no thanks to you.	*Something he has always had to do (see Chapter 3)*

NURSE	I am very concerned that you are risking yourself injury as well as others. I feel it is my responsibility, with my colleague here, to let you know our concern. You are well over the legal limit and we...	*Be clear with him. There is a witness present.*
MR J.	Go to hell *(storms out)*.	*I can't take any more of this.*

An ugly situation to be left with but, realistically, there is nothing more that can be done while he is this drunk – an important realisation for any talker faced with this situation.

This does not mean that nothing has been achieved, more that this was not the right time or place for the drinker to engage in the help he really needs. Exactly the right steps were taken in the context in which Mr Jocelyn chose to present his 'problem'. All too commonly, and sadly, the drinker asks for help in the very way in which he cannot get what he needs. However, he has probably taken a small step towards recognising this, which may enable him to move towards accepting help some time in the future.

A situation like this raises important issues about staff morale, cohesion and support. The talker may feel a huge mixture of feelings after such a dialogue – exhaustion, fear, frustration, helplessness, abuse. She dealt with the situation with remarkable skill, and needs time to resolve her feelings to enable her to work with such clarity and sensitivity again. Without this, her unresolved feelings may become entrenched. That is the cycle of prejudice. For further discussion, please refer to Chapter 5.

CHAPTER 10

'Disintegration' – Where All Areas of Life Are At Risk

Dialogue (1) Assessing Physical Dependence

Scene

A 54-year-old man, Richard Day, is referred to a specialist treatment unit and seen by a member of staff on the unit. He has been working as a clerk in a bank, but has failed to gain promotion and has had considerable time off work.

The GP was concerned about the contrast in descriptions of day-to-day difficulties. Mr Day states that things are unchanged, whilst his wife suggests that he has become restless and agitated, with increasing inability to look after himself. He is known to be a social drinker, with no obvious evidence of alcohol misuse but he was referred for help after being found drunk at home. His blood tests show some abnormal liver functioning (see Chapter 4).

Because of the contrasting picture described, and because of Mr Day's rather vague manner, the talker, in this assessment, has chosen to begin the interview with Mr and Mrs Day together.

Sensitive judgment may be needed to decide how best to proceed. It is important that Mr Day has an opportunity to represent himself at some stage in the assessment process.

Mr L.	Good morning. My name is Mr Lang. Thank you for coming to see me.	*Be gentle, encouraging and companionable. They may be scared (see Chapter 4).*
Mrs D.	Thank you for sparing the time.	*Perhaps worried that she is 'being a nuisance' and may not be taken seriously.*
Mr D.	That's fine.	
Mr L.	I'd like to ask you both some questions, to see what the difficulties are.	

Mrs D.	*(jumping in quickly)* He is a completely different man to what I married. He is so dreamy one minute and then the next he cannot sit still.	*Seems very keen to make her point. Feels anxious and bewildered.*
Mr L.	OK. And what about you, Mr Day? What has brought you along here today?	*Important to get an impression of both sides of the story.*
Mr D.	My doctor seemed to think it was a good idea.	*Detached and flat.*
Mr L.	What exactly do you think he was concerned about?	*Try and explore his understanding.*
Mr D.	Something to do with time off work.	*Making some connections.*
Mr L.	I see you have been having some time off, but I gather you have not been feeling too good recently.	*Confirm his perception. Continue to look for further insights.*
Mr D.	I'm fine. Look at me!	*Unable to recognise possible underlying complications.*
Mrs D.	Oh no you're not, Richard. This is what you always say. Last night you were pacing the house like a caged lion.	*Feels irritable, impatient and exasperated.*
Mr D.	No-one seems to understand. They do not have enough work for me recently. I've just been getting bored.	*Feels somewhat cornered. Can perhaps recognise that he is failing.*
Mr L.	I think our task today is to try and understand what is happening. How long have you been feeling bored at work?	*Try and keep alongside him. The helper may begin to feel some of Mrs D's exasperation.*
Mr D.	Um! Not long. But you know what it is like. I've been doing this job for a long time. I can do it without thinking.	*Plausible answer, which may be hiding a multitude of problems. Easy to be deceived by this.*

Mrs D.	Richard, you know you have been finding it more and more difficult. You have been given less and less to do because you cannot manage.	*'I just wish you would tell the truth!'*
Mr D.	Is that so?	*Holding the implied criticism at bay.*
Mr L.	How do you think things have changed, Mrs Day?	*Explore her perceptions rather than what she 'hears'.*
Mrs D.	He cannot concentrate very well. He seems to get het up over such silly little things, which he then can't remember.	*Feels angry and impatient with him.*
Mr D.	What! I can remember things OK. *(getting more agitated)* I know it was this morning you asked me when we had that lovely holiday in Scotland!	*Agitation increases as he feels more confronted and more out of his depth.*
Mrs D.	Yes. That was 25 years ago. It is what happened one year ago that you can never remember.	*Remains accusative.*
Mr L.	I am wondering if this is how it is at home.	*Reflect back. Part of the task of an assessment is to help them see their problems.*
Mrs D.	I can tell you this is just the beginning!	*Hidden agendas.*

The helper has to bear in the mind that the task is to assess an alcohol problem. He has already gleaned that there is considerable tension at home of a somewhat accusatory defensive nature. While this is important information, it seems that the relationship between Mr and Mrs Day may impede further exploration of the extent of an alcohol problem, and it may be important, at this stage, to see them individually, to clarify individual perceptions and prevent Mr Day having to be defensive.

The helper has already gleaned that

- Mr Day has some organic damage, highlighted by the blood tests.
- he can respond plausibly with a little insight.
- he struggles with short term memory.

- he gets agitated and het up. Seems unable to reason.
- he is in a marriage that has some problems.
- there is no smell of alcohol.
- no obvious sign of intoxication.
- rapport difficult, but some eye contact.
- looks clean and tidy, but not over concerned.
- rather sloppy gait. Shuffles.
- Mrs Day sees the problem as 'his'.
- she feels impatient. Does this cover up some underlying guilt?
- she feels exasperated and perhaps needs help for herself.
- she is in a marriage that she feels frustrated with.
- she seems efficient and business like.

MR L.   I appreciate that things are difficult at home. Our task is to tease out whether alcohol has a role to play in adding to problems at home. It very commonly does. I would like to talk to you individually now. I can see that hearing from both of you will help me but I think I also need to hear from you one at a time. Then we can come together again. I'd like to start with Mr Day. Mrs Day, could you wait outside in the waiting room? We will be about three quarters of an hour.

Acknowledge the hint at difficulties, and the hidden agendas. The helper does not want to fall into the same role of accuser. That will maintain defensiveness.

It seems courteous to start with the 'identified' patient.

Interview with Mr Day

MR L.   So, can you help me by telling me any more about how life is for you?

A very open question but helpful to see how he responds.

MR D.   Life is all right.

Important for the talker to try and sort out why Mr Day is presenting in this way. Careful history taking will help to assess present condition and events leading up to his referral. Assumptions are easily made.

Mr L.	Can you remember where you are?	*Assess orientation*
Mr D.	My wife told me we were coming to an alcohol unit.	*Needs some guidance.*
Mr L.	Do you know what it is called?	
Mr D.	I can't remember.	*Confused.*
Mr L.	It's the Jacob Clinic. Are you aware of why you may need to come for help to an alcohol clinic?	*Help him clarify the facts. See if he is able to retain this information.*
Mr D.	They say I have been drinking.	*I don't understand what has been happening to me.*
Mr L.	When did you last have a drink?	*Is there denial, confusion, or memory impairment (see Chapter 1)? Talker needs to separate out these possibilities.*
Mr D.	A couple of days ago.	*I don't really know.*
Mr L.	And what did you have to drink?	*Clarify physical dependence or possible intoxication.*
Mr D.	A cinzano.	
Mr L.	So that is all you have had to drink in two days. Is this your usual pattern?	*Reflect back what he is saying to help in clarification. Feels like a sticky interview.*
Mr D.	Well, I'm not sure.	*Perhaps he does not feel strong enough to declare what he is consuming.*
Mr L.	Your doctor tells me he found you on the floor at home after you had had too much to drink.	*Is there denial, blackouts, loss of memory?*
Mr D.	Oh! I can't remember that.	*Seems lost.*
Mr L.	I am wondering if you may have forgotten what you have been drinking?	*Assess his response to this possibility.*

MR D.	Could be.	*He can't be clear. Talker needs to explore signs of physical dependence first to exclude intoxication and then explore signs of memory loss separately (see Chapter 1).*
MR L.	Are you eating?	*Signs of anorexia?*
MR D.	Not much. I've never been a big eater.	*Very plausible answer.*
MR L.	Do your trousers still fit or do you need a belt?	*Looking for weight change. Loss/increase.*
MR D.	They seem a bit loose.	
MR L.	Are you sleeping well?	*Is his sleep pattern disturbed?*
MR D.	I don't get much sleep. I pace about.	
MR L.	Do you have a drink during the night?	*Is his agitation due to blood alcohol levels that are falling or a feature depression, or dementing process, pre-senile or alcohol related? Keep asking questions for clarification.*
MR D.	Sometimes. It settles me.	
MR L.	Do you have a drink first thing in the morning?	*Clarify if blood alcohol levels are falling.*
MR D.	I usually wait till my wife goes out.	*Feels the need to be secretive.*
MR L.	And then you have a drink.	*Ask about his secrets.*
MR D.	Sometimes.	
MR L.	Why do you wait till your wife goes out?	
MR D.	Not sure. She watches what I do.	*Feels controlled. Perhaps he has to search for bottles.*

MR L.	Do you feel shaky in the morning, have difficulty holding a cup of tea?	*Does he allow himself to experience withdrawal?*
MR D.	I feel restless, pace up and down.	*Could be alcohol withdrawal.*
MR L.	Does this settle after a drink?	*Relief drinking to deal with withdrawals?*
MR D.	Yes.	
MR L.	Have you ever had a black out, when you cannot remember what happened the night before?	*He may well not be able to answer this because of his confusion, but this sort of memory loss relates specifically to signs of temporary neurological impairment due to heavy consumption of alcohol.*
MR D.	My memory has never been very good.	*Not very helpful for the talker but shows some capacity for insight.*
MR L.	Does your wife ever tell you that you have done things that you do not remember?	*Looking for more information concerning his memory.*
MR D.	Yes, but she tends to make a meal of things – over plays it.	*Is this understanding or a defensive response?*
MR L.	Have you ever had an epileptic fit?	*Indicates a rapid fall in blood alcohol level.*
MR D.	(*looks confused*) No. Nothing like that.	*I think I have got enough to cope with.*
MR L.	Do you experience any pins and needles or numbness in your hands?	*Looking for peripheral neuropathy.*
MR D.	Gripping things can be difficult at times.	
MR L.	And in your feet?	
MR D.	I've been less steady on my feet. I stagger sometimes. My wife says I'm drunk.	

MR L.	Do you know if you have problems with your liver?	*Can imply long term alcohol abuse.*
MR D.	I don't know of any.	
MR L.	I understand from your doctor that your liver is showing signs of damage.	*Be clear with the facts that are known.*
MR D.	Oh.	*It may be difficult for him to link his drinking with any damage. Seems genuinely surprised.*

The talker may, from what Mr Day has said, have ascertained some features of a picture of physical dependence on alcohol. Heavy alcohol abuse can cause temporary or permanent memory impairment, which may be the cause of Mr Day's confusion. Entrenched denial can not be discounted. He may also have a dementing illness, which may be complicated by the use of alcohol. More commonly, it is the apparent dementia that is seen as the problem. This is why it is so crucial to clarify the role alcohol may be playing by taking a comprehensive history.

For the purposes of this chapter, the interview continues to focus on Mr Day's memory difficulties.

MR L.	Can you remember my name?	
MR D.	Er...no.	*Could be anxiety at the moment of meeting.*
MR L.	Can you remember where you are?	*Testing short term memory as stated earlier in the interview.*
MR D.	Er...no. I think it is some sort of clinic.	
MR L.	My name is Mr Lang and we are at the Jacob Clinic. What is the date today?	*Orientate him. It will make him feel safer.*
MR D.	Er...June 6th *(quizzically)*	*He is about three weeks out of date.*
MR L.	Year?	
MR D.	Er...1990.	*Seems to be guessing. Important clue to a possible demented state.*

MR L.	Who is Prime Minister at the moment?	*Keep searching for a correct connection with time.*
MR D.	I think there is a new one.	*Trying to cover up his difficulties. Feels awkward.*
MR L.	Can you remember the old one?	*Give him another chance to clarify his thoughts.*
MR D.	Er… (*becomes silent and visibly more agitated*).	*Feels embarrassed. Important that he is not pressed too hard.*

Mr Day gets increasingly confused and agitated by the various memory and orientation tests asked of him. It may be inappropriate, even impossible, to continue to take a full social and family history. So the question for the talker is how best to start to help. Mr Day is not visibly withdrawing, shaking or sweating; he is not obviously intoxicated although he is confused, with specific memory difficulties. His blood tests show evidence of heavy alcohol consumption and an outside witness suggests that his drinking has been out of control. The role of alcohol can never be underestimated until clarified otherwise.

MR L.	Thank you for answering these questions. Do you have any questions?	
MR D.	Not at the moment.	
MR L.	I would like to talk to your wife. Shall we go and find her?	*Will he get lost if left alone? Ask someone to observe him, as this could be helpful information.*

Interview with Mrs Day

MR L.	Come in, Mrs Day.	
MRS D.	You have taken a long time!	*Feels impatient and maybe anxious about what has been said in her absence.*
MR L.	I am sorry it has felt like that. Perhaps you can tell me how you see things.	*Easy to feel defensive. Perhaps that is how Mr Day feels.*

Mrs Day describes how her husband is an only child, always been very cautious about life and has never really stretched himself, especially at work. He has been doing a job which is relatively easy for his intellectual capacity for many years, never risking promotion. He has always been easily worried. They have been married 'fairly' happily for twenty years, and have not been able to have children. Mrs Day sought treatment with no success. She describes her husband as having few friends.

In relation to his drinking, he began drinking at home, after work. In the last five years, she saw less and less of his drinking, but he became more irritable and agitated. She describes how she became more unhappy and confused. 'The only thing I could do, Mr Lang, was to offer him a drink. He didn't seem to be having much, so I thought it would quieten him down'. She seemed very surprised, even shocked when asked if she had ever considered that Mr Day had been continuing to drink, but in secret.

Mrs Day says she would only drink very occasionally – at weddings, or Christmas.

MR L.	You have obviously felt under considerable stress yourself.	*Help her to start to consider her needs. Extend appreciation for her dilemma to help her feel less alone.*
MRS D.	I didn't know what else to do.	*Feels alone and unsupported.*
MR L.	You must have felt very frustrated with him sometimes.	*Help her to see her contribution.*
MRS D.	Well, wouldn't you?	*'I don't want to talk about this.'*

Mrs Day is struggling with feelings that have become 'bottled up'. She may feel guilty that she has contributed to her husband's 'problem' by encouraging him to drink. This will increase her sense of impatience and distress. Because of the liver damage, the helper could assume that Mr Day's drinking never stopped. It became more secretive. When asked, Mrs Day could not support or entertain this assumption.

Many relatives do not know if members of their family are drinking. Mrs Day may well need some help with the issues that she has raised for herself and on her husband's behalf.

MR L.	I am sure that living with someone who does get agitated must be hard at times. Do you get any kind of support for yourself?	
MRS DAY	I go round for a chat to my neighbour from time to time, but someone has got to keep the house in order.	*'I am a bit scared to let go.' May be taking responsibility away from her husband.*

The talker can bear in mind the benefits of organisational support from Al-Anon. As she is wary, a personal visit to her house might be most appropriate.

Bringing Mr Day back into the interview –

MR L.   Mr Day, I have been talking to your wife, and it seems that you have been getting increasingly agitated over the last few years. I am concerned about this. In relation to drinking, she tells me that you have been drinking less during that time. However, I do need to point out that the blood tests do show considerable damage to your liver. I therefore cannot discount a possible link between the two. I would like to suggest that we admit you, Mr Day, to the clinic to help us all clarify the cause of the problem. At the same time, we need to consider the best way of helping you, Mrs Day, to feel better about things.

Mr Day was admitted to the clinic to be observed and assessed. Initially, he was agitated and confused as has been described at interview. His agitation increased and because of the possibility of developing a Korsakoff's psychosis, if left untreated, he was given high doses of Vitamin B1 (Thiamine). He became shaky and very sweaty over two or three days, eating little, showing some signs of alcohol withdrawal.

Once clear of the withdrawal symptoms, he remained confused and disorientated, and continued to take vitamins (Thiamine B1) to hold at bay any further signs of impending Korsakoffs Psychosis (see Chapter 1). The Wernicke-Korsakoff Syndrome is caused by vitamin deficiency. It affects a part of the brain called the periventricals. The symptoms of staggering gait, confusion, and neuritis with which Mr Day presented were recognised and treated early. This avoided long term memory deficit and the development of Korsakoff's Psychosis.

With termination of drinking, recovery of appetite and slow withdrawal of replacement medication, Mr Day became much less agitated, his thinking became clearer, his memory more accurate and his mood brighter. He will remain like this if he chooses not to return to drinking.

Mrs Day was personally introduced to an Al-Anon member to help her to gain the support she needs to prevent her own distress contributing to her husband's desire to recommence drinking. His attendance at AA could also be recommended.

Stage 2. Exploring Sobriety

Once at home, Mr and Mrs Day recognised that their situation had improved in some areas:

- Mr Day had become more reliable in carrying out simple tasks of personal hygiene.
- Mrs Day was more relaxed.
- Mr Day was easier to talk to.
- There had been no drinking.
- Mrs Day had attended some Al-Anon meetings and was feeling less isolated.

However, some new difficulties were emerging:

- Mr Day was ready for more freedom, but Mrs Day did not feel comfortable about this, fearing he would return to drinking.
- When Mr Day got het up, neither he nor Mrs Day could resort to alcohol. Neither could find a solution so there were still rows, probably more than previously.
- Mr Day had not returned to work and therefore financial difficulties were developing.

It is now three months since his admission and they had seen Mr L twice. All are agreed that he has not been drinking. They arrive at the clinic for an appointment and wish to be seen separately. Mr Day is seen first. He looks physically better, walking more confidently and yet looks tense and distressed.

MR L.   How are you today?

MR D.   Awful – I don't really know where to start. I'm making an enormous effort and I feel dreadful. I just want things to be normal. It cannot be alcohol that was my problem, otherwise I would be better by now. What is the point of making all this effort?

Feeling very demoralised, has expectations that things will change quickly. Feels frustrated and cross, and has no escape.

Mr L.	Yes, I can see that you are trying very hard. It must be frustrating that you can't feel the benefits. Can you identify what is good about the changes that have happened?	*Acknowledge the frustration. The talker can also want the 'problems' to go away. Very important not to rush through the processes that take place in sobriety. He may be mourning the loss of alcohol, and having to face the reality of his situation for the first time in years. It is vital he has a chance to work through these stages.*
Mr D.	I'm feeling better in the mornings... and I don't fall over any more. But so what! My wife will not let me do things... and we just row all the time. I feel like drinking and why shouldn't I?	*Can acknowledge some benefits but quickly weighed down by the difficulties he is experiencing masked by alcohol in the past. Feels defiant and a need to escape.*
Mr L.	I don't think that would be the right solution. I can hear that you feel cheated that even with all this effort, things have not come right. I can honestly say that things would be even worse if you started drinking again.	*Talker has to be able to give the drinker responsibility for his own actions, even if he expresses the desire to drink, as this is what his wife has such difficulty doing. Be straight. He needs something firm to hang on to.*
Mr D.	Not even the odd one? That's all I want – to feel normal – less lonely not on the scrap heap. Nobody respects me. I'm just a worn out old man – with my wife waiting for the first wrong move.	*Very low self esteem. Loss of all his roles, even that of a drinker. Grieving for the ideals of his drinking times.*

Mr Day is describing a situation that is very common. So often there is a belief that if the drinking stops, everything will fall into place. But patterns of behaviour and responses can be so well established that these have to change too. Drinking may have masked personal difficulties for many years. It is only when the drinking stops that these difficulties emerge for what they really are. They may have precipitated the heavy drinking in the first place.

The talker's task is to help Mr Day begin to face these issues as well as identify some goals which he can feel are his and to help him look at the structure necessary to achieve them. With help, he can see he has some daily structure.

Taking the dog out and visiting a neighbour on a regular basis may help to work towards a view to returning to some more structured work.

Negotiations with his boss may be a longer term goal, looking at the possibility of part time employment. He would like to go out and see people and suggests going to the pub. At this stage of sobriety, it is a very challenging task and can feed denial of the severity of the alcohol problem and create even greater stresses on the marital situation. It seems that attendance at Alcoholics Anonymous, for social contact and support, would be a more appropriate goal to discuss.

Interview with Mrs Day

MR L.   Come in, Mrs Day, I...

MRS D.   I expect Richard has told you how dreadful it is at home. He just mopes about all day. You would think he would have got better by now.

Also feels angry and disappointed with progress. Externalising the 'blame' onto husband and talker. Easy for the talker to feel that he is not doing enough.

MR L.   I understand things are still quite trying.

Hear what is being said, but do not pick up the blame.

MRS D.   Well, to be honest with you, at least I knew where we were when he was drinking. Now he wants to go to the pub and gets angry because I stop him. You'd think he'd be grateful for all the help I'm giving him. He says he will not drink but...

The relationship between them has not changed. The only difference is that there is no alcohol involved. A very difficult issue to face for both parties, although it becomes clear that it is the 'drinker' who takes the blame. Although both parties suffer.

MR L.   You need to allow yourselves some more time. Yes, the drinking has stopped but essentially, your relationship has stayed the same and will take time to change. It is important that your husband feels he can begin to take responsibility for some aspects of his life and for you not to feel you have to look after him.

Help her clarify some of her distress – another important step for them both towards true sobriety.

MRS D.   But how can I, with all that has happened?

Such is the strength of her despair. Needs support.

Whilst Mrs Day's struggle is also very real and commonly experienced, she has to realise that, in order for things to change, she will have to explore her own behaviour in relation to the marriage and not merely assume that Mr Day is at fault.

MR L.   What is the heaviest burden on
          you at the moment?

MRS D.   That I have to watch him all the   *Loss of trust and control.*
          time, just in case he goes back to
          his old ways.

MR L.   How could this be different?

MRS D.   Well, I'd have to trust him more.

MR L.   What has to happen before you
          can do that?

MRS D.   He needs to do more for himself.

MR L.   I think that is what he wants too.
          But you are going to have to
          take some risks, and this is
          where Al-Anon can really help
          you. He may not always do
          what you want!

Although Mr and Mrs Day seem to want different things, they are in fact struggling to find a new order, which is confusing and painful – Mrs Day needs to find a way of letting go of the sense that she has to be responsible for her husband and therefore prevent him from relapsing, while Mr Day has to accept that his behaviour in the past has caused others to worry and make decisions for him. If this is to change, he will need to demonstrate that his behaviour can be trustworthy.

Making a new order in a relationship is complex, will take time, and may well be hampered by relapse. This dialogue demonstrates only one small stage of the process. It is important for the talker to consider the connections between relationships to other individuals and to alcohol in order to help the drinker, and those around him through the long journey to sobriety.

Dialogue (2) Relapse and Petty Offending – Interview with Probation Officer

Scene

Middle-aged man (Tony), who has been drinking heavily for ten years and is separated from his wife and family, has latterly turned to theft, when intoxicated, to subsidise his drinking. He is on two years' probation for such offences and has just re-offended after a heavy bout of drinking. As a result, he may face a custodial sentence. He has been to prison before and is appalled at the prospect of returning.

This scene describes an interview with his Probation Officer, (Andrew) whom Tony has known for some eighteen months, and with whom he has a good relationship. Before the drinking bout, Tony had been sober for six months and had been living in supportive accommodation. At interview, he has stopped drinking, but feels full of remorse, regret and despondency.

TONY	*(head in hands)* Well, I have well and truly blown it this time, haven't I?	*Feels guilty, and angry, and looking for confirmation of self rejection.*

The most crucial stage of this interview comes at the beginning. Both parties are struggling with their individual emotional responses to the changed situation, and for both parties the feelings may be the same – frustration, anger, quilt, failure, shock, helplessness, despair. However, relapse, for the drinker, can be time for change and learning. Some of that change can be facilitated by the response of the talker to the drinker's perceived failure and helplessness, and to his own feelings of frustration, anger and despair.

As the opening of the dialogue suggests, the drinker will be looking for reinforcement from the talker of his self rejection and punishment as a justification to perpetuate his 'drinking'. The drinker will be angry – turned inwards in remorse, and/or outwards in blame. It is important for the talker (Andrew) to address the feelings that the situation arouses in him (see Chapter 5) and to be clear what is helpful for Tony.

ANDREW	What do you mean, 'blown it?'	*Reflect back his question for Tony to make his own assessment. Do not deny or collude with his perceptions.*
TONY	Well, I have done it, haven't I?	*Still wants to hide in his shame and not face things.*
ANDREW	I think you need tell me what 'it' is.	*He wants rescuing from his pain. It will not help him to pull him out of it – that is what alcohol does.*

Help him to face himself so that he will find his own strengths.

TONY   You know I have been on a bender.

He may be hoping that the talker will say things for him.

ANDREW I can see that you have been drinking. You look pretty rough.

Be clear. Sympathy is hard to take and can block expression.

TONY   Rough!! Christ, I feel like death!
                    silence

Releasing some despair.
Let Tony reflect.

TONY   And I was doing so well... Look where I am now. Back to square one!
                    (looks up at Andrew)
                    You're not saying much!

Feels intense failure.

Needs to feel support and contact.

ANDREW I'm listening. My hunch is that anything I say will make you feel worse.

State presence and reflect back the punishment he is seeking.

TONY   Will I have to go back to prison?

Picks up the association with the guilt.

ANDREW You obviously feel very guilty.

Help him make this connection.

TONY   Well, put it this way, I wish I had never done it!

Difficult to be direct with his feelings.

ANDREW You still have not told me what IT is. Tell me what happened.

Read the non-verbal cues he is giving.

TONY   I was desperate for a drink. I put a brick through a shop window and pinched some booze. The police were there in a trice and tried to get it off of me. The b...s were so rough. I slugged the young un'.
                    pause
                    What do you think is going to happen to me?

Indicates level of addiction and desperateness. Feels very scared.

ANDREW Well, the truth is that I don't know. You have re-offended several times and a sentence depends on so many things. But what I do know is that you do not offend when you are sober. I think we need to concentrate on helping you achieve and maintain sobriety. That will keep you out of trouble and help things look more favourable in court.

Be straight. Do not give false hopes as he must face up to the consequences of his actions.

TONY   It's when I see the other blokes. I can't walk away.

Feels helpless and not certain he wants to take responsibility.

ANDREW Are you saying you don't want to be dry?

Don't rescue him from his helplessness as that will increase dependency on the talker and what the drinker is seeking. Face the drinker with his own responsibility.

TONY   Oh Christ, Yes! I just find it bloody difficult when others around me are drinking.

Defensive of his own ambivalence but able to acknowledge his struggle.

ANDREW What about changing where you live?

TONY   That means living on my own and you know what *that* means.

Still feels a bit despairing and helpless. He is very scared and is throwing out a line to be rescued from his fear.

ANDREW You seem to be very scared.

Don't catch the line. Feed back his sentiments.

TONY   Well, I'm scared of blowing it yet again!

Can begin to recognise his needs.

ANDREW What do you think might help?

Help him set some reasonable goals.

| TONY | Oh I don't know. You are supposed to be the expert. | *Trapped in his own angry dependency, feels passive and unable to take responsibility, yet feels deeply resentful of this (see Chapter 3).* |

This is another crucial stage of the interview, as it would be easy for the talker to get sucked into the pessimism and helplessness of the drinker. This perhaps suggests the degree of entrenchment of dependency of the drinker's personality, and often the point where many talkers feel most frustrated, feel like giving up, getting angry – and/or taking control and becoming the expert. The drinker expresses his helplessness by forcing the talker to feel equally trapped.

It is at the point of feeling trapped that the talker feels like freeing themselves from the overwhelming needs of the drinker – and commonly does, either by removing themselves emotionally (albeit unconsciously), feeling defeated and turning the sense of helplessness back onto the drinker; 'He is a waste of time, he will never change' (see Chapter 4), or by absorbing the overwhelming dependency and beginning to do everything to protect the vulnerability of the drinker and the talker.

It is vital for the health of both parties that each acknowledge that they may feel helpless, defeated and fearful. Balancing out the emotional responses allows space for hope, and with hope can come change. Part of that hope rests with the reality that the drinker retains the right to choose whether to stay dry or to drink. It is the authors' experience that it is impossible to predict who will stay dry and who will return to drinking. It is the suspension of that prediction that can enable the drinker to retain the choice.

It may be important for the talker to accept that people like Tony may always be vulnerable to drink and relapse in certain stressful situations. Looking at triggers for drinking and looking at response patterns may help Tony come to terms with possible relapse.

The responsibility of the drinker is to face the emotional and practical consequences of his choice. The responsibility of the talker is to help the drinker explore his choice, and if he wants to attempt sobriety, to help define mutually acceptable perimeters that support the drinker towards a goal that is agreeable to both parties. If the goal-posts are out of line, the goal is unattainable. In Tony's case, he knows that if he drinks, he will re-offend (see Chapter 3).

Therefore, his aim must be abstinence from alcohol. In order to help him achieve this, he needs to be in a setting in which he feels safe to begin to work at his fears, anxieties and confidence. The ensuing dialogue may demonstrate an approach.

ANDREW	Well, I think we are both experts at different things. It feels as if you have lost your strength and are looking for that in me. I think you know that relapse adds to experience.	*Be open, reflecting back what is happening without rejecting.*
TONY	All I am good at is bloody drinking.	*Still feels very hopeless.*
ANDREW	Shall we look at ways that can be different? I don't entirely agree with the last statement. You were sober for six months before this last fling, and you managed to stop. You are not drinking now, and you are indicating to me that you want to stay sober. Am I right?	*Clarify the reality for the drinker. In his hopelessness, he loses sight of any goal-posts.*
TONY	Well I haven't got a choice. Otherwise I really will go down.	*Not quite grasping full responsibility.*
ANDREW	Lots of people go to prison.	*Don't take his responsibility.*
TONY	Yeah – OK... I suppose you are saying I can do something for myself.	*Feeling stronger.*
ANDREW	Let's look at the options open to us and then, after the court case, we can reconsider. You can stay where you are, and risk being tempted to drink with the lads; we can try and find you a hostel that is dry. What do you think?	
TONY	I want to stay where I am. Mrs W. has been very good to me. I might ask her if I could have the front room on my own. But I get so bored during the day!	*Beginning to solve own problems, but also expressing his own needs.*
ANDREW	Well, let's stick to that, and as I say, review after the court case. I suggest you come to the	

> probation day centre a few times
> in the week, meet others, and we
> can talk some more.

TONY   OK.

No dialogue is ever complete. The interaction will remain with the two partici-
pants in whatever way they have experienced that interaction, be it hopeful,
sad, frustrated, and so forth. Such experiences will become the fruits of the next
dialogue. It is always tempting for the talker to offer something practical to the
drinker as a 'reward'. This can be appropriate, but commonly it is a defence
against the talker's feelings of powerless and uselessness. The result is that it
renders the drinker once again powerless, but now carrying the powerlessness
of the talker. In the above dialogue it is vital that Tony talks to his landlady
himself, and Andrew does not offer to do it for him.

It may also be important to address why Tony relapsed at that time. Sometimes individuals cannot sustain sobriety or 'doing well' because help gets
withdrawn. Relapse is a way of expressing the fear that support may disappear.

Stage 2. Issues encountered in sobriety

Six months have passed since Tony's relapse. He has looked carefully at triggers
to his drinking. He has identified that certain times of the year – his wife's
birthday and memories of his children are still difficult for him. He often
wonders if he should just forget or whether he should be sorting himself out so
that he can make contact with them again.

He does not feel good about himself or his prospects for the future. Just as
soon as he begins to make progress, he seems to get a knock and does not think
he will ever get out of the homeless, unemployed, dependent cycle which
ultimately makes being 'dry' very hard for him. Drinking gives him status.
Without it, he sees himself as having nothing.

After the court case, he is having a discussion with Andrew.

TONY   It's just so hard. The options are   *Feels despairing and lost, perhaps*
          very few if you don't drink.   *how he felt as a child. Trapped,*
                                                       with little direction.

ANDREW What do you mean?   *Don't be scared by the threat of*
                                                       relapse. Important that he is helped
                                                       to clarify his options.

TONY	Well, you're never really alone when you are drinking. You can usually find someone to share your time with. If you're on your own, it's so much harder. There are people like you, but they all have homes to go to. It is hard to make friends if you have no money and you cannot drink. I have nothing to talk about except bloody drink.	*Some truth in this, but idealised sense of what drink will provide. Difficulty of taking risks to change lifestyle yet lonely and empty, perhaps the very cause of original drinking behaviour.*
ANDREW	Yes, but you seem to have chosen that path rather than risk something else.	*Important not to get trapped with the drinker. Rigidity and fear seem to be holding Tony back, suggesting some need for psychological change.*
TONY	What do you mean?	
ANDREW	Well, you have managed to stay dry, but you are very lonely. It is not just as simple as the drink.	*He needs to begin to tackle his interaction with the larger world.*
TONY	That's all that I have known for so long now.	*'I don't know that I can be different'.*
ANDREW	Changing the way we do things can be pretty frightening, but I think you are ready to have a go.	*Encouragement and confidence in the drinker will help him feel less stuck. May feel risky but very important for self esteem.*
TONY	What should I change?	*Feels lost and rather out of his depth. Needs some clear guidance – perhaps he has never had this before.*

ANDREW	For things to be different, we need to think about your lifestyle, and see if there are ways of developing your interests, bringing you in contact with others, even to consider living with others in the same situation.	*Needs clarity and a bit of a push.*
TONY	Oh no not that again. You seem to think that going to a dry house is the answer.	*Wary of taking risks. Difficulty in embracing responsibility.*
ANDREW	From what I know of you and of them, I think something like that may have a lot to offer – support, companionship, a challenge, meeting others who are not drinkers.	*Help him to see the benefits. Beware of the frustration aroused by his resistance. Working with this defence is an important part of promoting change.*
TONY	I can stay dry. I don't need that sort of thing.	*Fearful*
ANDREW	I know you can stay dry, and that is to your credit, but everything else in your life stays the same. You need to decide whether you want to keep repeating the same pattern of getting lonely and miserable and risking relapse. Why not give it some thought. We can always arrange a visit and talk to others about the idea.	*Be clear, without taking the responsibility for him. That will prevent real change.*
TONY	What about my freedom! I will not be told what to do.	*Scared of feeling trapped, 'Independence' can often mask an enormous fear of emotional dependency – that is translated into drinking.*

ANDREW	I can understand that, but let's face it, some of the choices you have made in the past have not been ones that you have managed for long. And then you return to situations where others make decisions for you – like myself.	*Don't be thrown off track. He does that for himself. He needs objectivity and clarity to help him make clear decisions.*
TONY	I think that is a bit tough!	*Very hard to face up to the truth.*
ANDREW	Well, I think a bit of frank talking is what is needed right now.	*Needs help. Don't be diverted by his resistance and fear.*
TONY	So what happens if I don't do what you want!	*Responds with some defiance rebellion – again a protection against fear.*
ANDREW	Your Probation Order means that we need to meet regularly, but I cannot insist on more than that.	*Be clear with boundaries. Hand back the responsibility. He wants you to back down, so that he might have someone to blame if things go wrong.*
TONY	I think I will stay where I am. Maybe I could go with Alan to the river, and see about some fishing. I used to enjoy that. Ah! all the gear I used to have! Any chance of help to get some more?	*Finding his own ideas and spontaneous solutions.*
ANDREW	We used to have some at the day centre. I'll have a look. Meanwhile, just check out some second hand shops, or what the basics cost and we'll take it from there.	*Important to respond to Tony's idea, even if it is different from that of the talker, as he can embrace it as his own. Vital for self esteem.*
TONY	I think he belongs to some sort of club…	*Beginning to see further than before.*
ANDREW	OK, it sounds as if we will have plenty to talk about when we meet in two weeks' time.	*Maintain confidence by establishing a commitment to this idea.*

Tackling issues in sobriety can seem as difficult and frustrating as when drinking is involved for both the talker and the drinker. It is vital, therefore, to discuss expectations and goals that are realistic and mutually held. Resentments, misunderstandings and frustrations on the part of the talker can get transferred back to the drinker and can unwittingly contribute to potential relapse. Likewise fear of relapse can prevent progress and induce dependency (see Chapters 3 and 4).

CHAPTER 11

'Turning Points' – The Dilemmas of Change

Dialogue (1) Interview with Social Worker

Scene

Doris is a 78-year-old woman who lives alone and receives most of her practical and emotional support from a home help and a social worker. Members of her family live nearby, but there is little contact and relationships are somewhat strained.

The conversation with her social worker (Ruth) takes place in an acute medical ward of a large general hospital, two days after admission. As she is somewhat deaf, it takes place with raised voices and with little hope of much privacy or confidentiality.

RUTH	Well, hello, Doris.	
DORIS	You've taken a long time to come and see me.	*Feels needy but angry. Very open about her demands (see Chapter 3).*
RUTH	Only a couple of days. Do you know how long you have been here for, Doris?	*Talker rather thrown aback by her frankness.*
DORIS	You've just told me, a couple of days.	*Hostility disguised in humour.*
RUTH	Yes, and do you know why you are here?	*She is clearly 'on the ball'. Important to find out what she understands.*
DORIS	Well, I just took the pills that the doctor gave me.	*Unable to face the responsibility for her actions.*

RUTH	Mmm, but you took them all at the same time; the whole bottle.	*Keep her to the reality of the situation.*
DORIS	No (*with disbelief*) no.	
RUTH	It's true – and there was a bottle of vodka by your bed.	
DORIS	Well, you know I have a drink. I mean, there's not much to do when you live on your own and you are nearly eighty.	*Underneath, she must be feeling very empty.*
RUTH	The trouble is, Doris, it is very dangerous.	*The talker feels considerable concern, and perhaps some helplessness, even exasperation.*
DORIS	What do you mean it's dangerous. I have been drinking all my life.	*Denial continues, putting forward strong rationalisation.*
RUTH	You are putting your life greatly at risk, taking so many pills with a lot of drink...	*Strength of the defence creates firm response from talker.*
DORIS	Ooh!	*Seems surprised at this suggestion.*
RUTH	Does that not worry you?	*Will she take some responsibility for her behaviour?*
DORIS	We women in this family, we're all very strong.	*'I have no intention of changing'*
RUTH	That's true, but...	
DORIS	(*interrupts*) But if only my family visited me a bit more, things would be all right.	*Feels lonely, angry and rejected.*
RUTH	Do you think that is perhaps why you did it?	*Help her to keep opening up.*
DORIS	Well, I'm lonely.	*Insight.*
RUTH	I know, I know (*softly*) We have discussed the idea of going to visit centres during the day.	*Be cautious not to be punitive, as she feels that everybody else is.*

DORIS	But, they are all so old, they just sit there and stare; they don't speak. There is no life there.	*Can't bear to face up to herself and her true situation.*
RUTH	You worry me, Doris. I know you are lonely, I know your relatives don't come very often – but by doing what you have just done, is going to make that all much worse. I think your family are thinking 'what can we do now; we've tried our best and there's nothing…'	*Mirror image – Doris is giving up, (i.e., by drinking) as family is giving up on her.*
DORIS	(interrupts) They want to put me away in a home. They want to take everything away from me.	*Disarmingly truthful, but will not take responsibility for herself and puts the blame on others.*
RUTH	They want to make sure you are safe.	
DORIS	Oh yes, so they don't even have to worry about coming to see me, that's just fine.	*Feels abandoned.*
RUTH	Well, I can see why you see it like that. But the reality is that you are an old lady and you have put your life greatly at risk.	
DORIS	Well, I am going to die soon anyway, and I want to be in my own home and look after myself.	*Clearly asserting her position and rights.*

There is a real dilemma facing the talker at this stage. The feelings expressed of hopelessness, despair and frustration with the situation are mutually held. If this lady was not a drinker, would she be facing the prospect of a home? Conversely, if she were a younger person and drinking, there would be little debate about providing an environment which might go some way to protect her from accessibility to alcohol. Does she not have the right to retain the responsibility for her drinking despite her age? Is she not as much at risk of self-harm as a young lad getting badly hurt in a brawl? The issue of responsibility seems crucial. The responsibility of the talker is to help the drinker understand her drinking and the consequences that arise as a result. If responsibility is assumed, plans will fail and drinking is likely to continue. In this dialogue, the talker has to face the drinker with some difficult choices and help her come to terms with them.

RUTH	Because of your actions in the last couple of days you have shown that there is a part of you that does not want to look after yourself. And that is why we are sitting here.	
DORIS	Well, can't one of my children have me to live with them?	*There is part of her that does badly want to be looked after.*
RUTH	I think you know that that wouldn't work.	*Don't get side-tracked by unreasonable ideas to please her.*
DORIS	Well, what would work then!	*Feels angry and rejected.*
RUTH	I think we need to look around and find a place where you would feel comfortable and at home.	*Share the task and thus the responsibility.*
DORIS	So you're saying that if I found somewhere and I don't like it, then I don't have to go?	*Needs to retain some esteem.*
RUTH	Well, I think it is reasonable to say that the choice to live on your own is now out of the question, but that you can have some choice as to where you will live.	
DORIS	I've lived in that house… (*mumbles into silence*).	*Some resignation.*
RUTH	I know it's distressing. I wouldn't like to be in your shoes.	*Acknowledge her shift of mood.*
DORIS	Wouldn't fit you anyway! (*smiles*) Is my daughter coming to visit me?	

RUTH	I have told her where you are and I have also told her and I will tell you, that she can see you on the understanding she does not bring you any alcohol.	*It becomes clear that Doris's shift of mood is connected with the prospect of getting a drink. Such is the entrenchment of the problem.*
DORIS	What?	*The denial returns.*
RUTH	This is a hospital.	
DORIS	Look, I know that beer is good for you. It builds you up. I am not asking for anything special, just a drop of brandy maybe.	*Pleading, seductive, helpless just as she is with her family.*
RUTH	Doris, this is a hospital, you have just taken a serious overdose. You seem unable to grasp the seriousness of your situation and it is exactly for this reason we have to find you somewhere safe to live.	*Remain firm and clear.*
DORIS	I can't drink anymore, is that what you are saying?	*Passing the responsibility and the blame to the talker.*
RUTH	Yes.	
DORIS	How are you going to make me not drink?	
RUTH	I can't make you not drink. It is my suggestion that you think of your life without alcohol.	
DORIS	So if you put me in a home then I won't be able to drink? I will never be happy. My mother used to say that a little milk stout didn't hurt.	*Finding reasons to justify her position.*
RUTH	Your mother was not an alcoholic, Doris.	*Keep to task.*

DORIS	*(laughing in disbelief)* Alcoholic? I don't need a drink, I just like a drink.	*Entrenched denial.*
RUTH	… and it makes you very ill.	
DORIS	*(thoughtful)* So what sort of place can I go to that I can be happy in, where I can't drink and where it won't be lined with old fuddy-duddies?	*Some reality is dawning but it feels very unacceptable.*
RUTH	It's not an easy business, I know that.	*Recognise her struggle.*
DORIS	So this is what the doctors saved me for. I wish I were dead. *Pause*	*Expression of real despair.*
RUTH	You must be wondering what is the point of going on for an old person like yourself, if you see the future as so gloomy.	*This may well be in the mind of the talker, who can also get overwhelmed by helplessness (see Chapter 5) It is vital the talker instigates some hope while recognising the despair.*
DORIS	Yes, precisely. If you send me home, I'll be all right.	*Different foundations for hope.*

This request clearly leaves the social worker with a dilemma. When the client's perception of needs are so at variance with those of the helper, who is right? How one uses one's influence in this situation may well be dependent on resources available; will sheltered accommodation be available even if it is acceptable? What will happen if things go wrong? Will the talker be supported by her supervisor?

There is also the loss of independence for the client at stake and an understandably tenacious desire to hang on to what is left. So often one hears comments about the elderly such as:

'They have so little to look forward to, why not let them drink.'

'If I had her life I'd be drinking too.'

'Why shouldn't they have some fun.'

The talker must embrace these dilemmas in order to promote change.

Dialogue (2) A Homeless Man talks to a Volunteer at a hostel
Scene

A 56-year-old man, Frank, has been drinking since his late teens, very heavily for the last ten years, living rough and moving from town to town. His tolerance to alcohol is now very low (see Chapter 1), and he has just completed a distressing withdrawal period because his body could not tolerate any more alcohol. He is searching for some accommodation that will accept him, and in this dialogue, he is talking to Jane, who has just shown him around a hostel for homeless men.

JANE	So what do you think of this place?	
FRANK	Not bad, not bad. Everybody looks a bit fed up.	*Suggests his own misery seen in others.*
JANE	At least they are not drinking.	*Instil some hope.*
FRANK	You mean you are not allowed to drink here!	*Seeking permission to continue old habits.*
JANE	No. In fairness to those that want to stop, we ask everybody not to drink.	*Don't be swayed by this challenge.*
FRANK	But my mate Billy drank when he was here.	*Feels very uncertain about stopping drinking. Personifying his drinking self in another.*
JANE	Well, I don't know Billy but I do know that it would help you if you stopped. Otherwise, we both know it is going to get the better of you.	*Don't fall into the trap of discussing others. It can be avoiding the issue for both parties. Be direct but considerate. The drinker is very scared.*
FRANK	But what's the point. I may as well die happy as miserable.	*Feels as though he is facing an impossible task. Disguises feelings through humour.*

It is easy for the talker and the drinker to get bogged down by such statements, perhaps because of the identification with the 'truths' of the words. It is important for the talker to reflect to the drinker the ambiguity of his words – he is not drinking and he is seeking a place to live that takes him off the streets.

JANE	I don't think that is entirely true. I think you must want to get off the streets if you are looking for somewhere to live.	
FRANK	But what is the alternative? I get wrecked if I drink and miserable if I don't. All my friends are drinkers. I haven't seen my family in years.	*Feels very confused and uncertain which way to turn.*
JANE	I think your body is telling you that you can't drink anymore.	*Help to clarify the facts.*
FRANK	But John is older than me and he is still going strong. He has been on the meths for years.	*Avoiding the issue by seeing his drinking self in others. Feels envious.*
JANE	Frank, you are not John. You feel envious but you have a different body and a different mind. He has made his choice. You make yours.	*Easy for the talker to get swamped by the strong feelings of helplessness. Keep to task to help with the drinker's confusion.*
FRANK	Well, I haven't got anywhere else to go.	*Has to face the reality of his situation. Feels resentful.*

This could be a point of collusion for the talker. She may think that Frank does not have anywhere to go. Commonly, the talker's identification with the despair and hopelessness of such a situation forces them to 'join ranks' with the drinker and 'put the blame' (and the pain) outside themselves onto another anonymous entity (commonly, the housing department, the government, etc). Although this energy is very useful for political purposes, to strive for change, it is important not to drag the drinker into the same net.

Frank has made choices throughout his life (albeit choices that have been clouded by apparently insurmountable factors) for him to be in the position he is now in. To help him with his right to choose has to be the purpose of the task. To deny choice depletes self-esteem. The talker has to be bold and help the drinker clarify his options for his own self-esteem.

JANE	You could always go back to the streets.	*Paradoxical statements can help the drinker explore alternative options.*

FRANK	Well put it this way. I haven't got anywhere better to go!	*Expressing some choice and some despair.*
JANE	I realise that. Well, give it a go and see how you settle in. Have you been in a hostel before?	*Help him explore his reservations.*
FRANK	Oh these places are all the same! I've tried dozens of them and they all have the same petty rules, you must do this, you can't do that!	*His repeated failure is defended by his hostile attitude toward help.*
JANE	(*stays quiet*)	

It may be important for the drinker to express some of his rage and hostility. It will make him feel safer if the talker can accept feelings. It is also important for the talker not to avoid his hostility by making the place on offer sound 'better'. It is easy to seduce people into making a choice as it can reward the talker by becoming the 'provider'. Drinkers need to rebel against the providers, as a defence against their own dependency and unobtained needs.

It is vital that the drinker makes his own choice with whatever information about resources he has to hand. In the light of this, it is important to make clear what is being provided, so that the drinker can clarify his choice. The drinker often puts himself in the wrong place to get the help he needs and it is therefore crucial for the talker to acknowledge the limitations of an institution rather than face the drinker with yet another failure should he accept but then be unable to stay.

JANE	There are two main rules here. No drinking or abusing drugs, and no violence to others or property. If that happens we ask you to leave. Otherwise we are fairly easy going. It is a start. Some go on to find their own accommodation. Some seem happy to stay for as long as they like. What do you think?	*Restore hope.*
FRANK	OK, I'll give it a try.	

References

Anderson, P. (1983) 'Alcohol'. In S. Lock (ed.) *Practising Prevention*. London: British Medical Association.

Bennett, T. and Wright, R. (1984) 'The relationship between alcohol use and burglary'. *British Journal of Addiction 79*, 431–37.

Berlin, N. (1982) *Eugene O'Neill*. Basingstoke: Macmillan Press Ltd.

Blane, H. (1968) *The Personality of the Alcoholic; Guises of Dependency*. New York: Harper and Rowe.

Blum, E.M. (1966) 'Psycho-analytic views on alcoholism – a review'. *Quarterly Journal of Studies on Alcoholism, 27*, 259–299.

Borg, S. (1978) *Homeless Men. A clinical and social study with special reference to alcohol abuse.* Acta Psychologica Scandinavica Supplementum 276.

British Association of Occupational Therapists (1990) *Code of Professional Conduct*. London: College of Occupational Therapists.

British Medical Association (1988) *The Drinking Driver*. Report of the Board of Science and Education.

Burnham, J.B. (1988) *Family Therapy: First Steps Towards a Systemic Approach*. London: Routledge.

Cadoret, R.J. , Cain, C.A. and Grove, W.M. (1980) 'Development of alcoholism in adoptees raised apart from alcoholic, biologic relations'. *Archives of General Psychiatry. 37*, 561–563.

Cassel, J. (1976) 'The contribution of the social environment to host resistance'. *American Journal of Epidemiology 104*, 107–123.

Dight, S. (1976) *Scottish Drinking Habits*. London: HMSO.

Edwards, G. (1982) *The Treatment of Drinking Problems – a Guide for the Helping Professions*. London: Grant McIntyre.

Edwards, G. (1974) 'Drugs, drug dependency and the concept of plasticity'. *Quarterly Journal of Studies on Alcohol 34*, 28–56.

Erikson, E. (1950) *Child and Society*. New York: W.W. Norton and Co. Inc.

General Household Survey (1990) Office of Population Censuses and Surveys 1992.

Gillies, H. (1976) 'Homocide in the West of Scotland'. *British Medical Journal 128*, 105– 27.

Goodwin, D.W. (1979) 'Alcoholism and heredity'. *Archives of General Psychiatry. 36*, 57–61.

Hawkins, P. and Shohet, R. (1989) *Supervision in the Helping Professions*. Milton Keynes: Open University Press.

Hore, B. (1976) *Alcohol Dependence*. London: Butterworth.

Jacobs, M. (1986) *The Presenting Past*. Milton Keynes: Open University Press.

Jacob, T. and Seilhamer, R.A. (1982) 'The impact on spouses and how they cope'. In J. Orford and J. Harwin (eds) *Alcohol and the Family*. London: Croom Helm.

Jellinek, E.M. (1960) *The Disease Concept of Alcoholism*. New Haven: Hill House Press.

Jessor, R. and Jessor, S.L. (1975) 'Adolescent development and the onset of drinking'. *Journal of Studies on Alcohol 36*, 27–51.

Kessel, N. and Walton, H. (1989) *Alcoholism*. London: Penguin.

McCord, W. and McCord J. (1960) *Origins of Alcoholism*. Stanford: Stanford University Press.

Macloed, G., Mayfield, D. and Hay, P. (1972) 'The CAGE questionnaire – validation of a new alcoholism screening test'. *American Journal of Psychology 129*, 342–345.

Marlatt, G.A., Demming, B. and Reid, J.B. (1973) 'Loss of control drinking in alcoholics: An experimental analogue'. *Journal of Abnormal Psychology 84*, 652–659.

Masserman, J.H. and Yum, K.S. (1946) 'An analysis of the influence of alcohol on experimental neurosis in cats'. *Psychosomatic Medicine. 8*, 36–52.

Masserman, J.H., Yum, K.S. *et al.* (1944) 'Neurosis and alcohol: an experimental study'. *American Journal Psychiatry 101*, 389–395.

Mello, N.K. (1972) 'Behavioural Studies of Alcoholism'. In B. Kissin and H. Begleiter (ed) *Physiology and Behaviour, The Biology of Alcoholism, Vol 2.* New York: Plenum Press.

Mello, N.K. and Mendleson, J.H. (1972) 'Drinking patterns during work – contingent and noncontingent alcohol acquisitions'. *Psychosomatic Medicine 34*, 139–164.

Mendleson, J.H. and Mello, N.K. (1979) 'Biological concomitants of alcoholism'. *New England Journal of Medicine 301*, 912–921.

Menninger K.M. (1938) *Man Against Himself.* New York: Harcourt Brace.

Merikanges K.R. (1990) 'The genetic epidemiology of alcoholism'. *Psychological Medicine 20. 1*, 11–22.

Mulry, J. (1987) 'Co-dependency – A family addiction'. *American Family Physician, 35, 4,* 215–219.

Platt, S. (1983) 'Parasuicide'. Paper presented to the First Scottish School in Drug Problems. Edinburgh: Herriot-Watt University.

Riley, D. (1984) 'Drivers' beliefs about alcohol and the law'. *Home Office research Bulletin.* No 17. London: Home Office.

Royal College of Physicians (1987) *The Medical Consequences of Alcohol Abuse: A Great and Growing Evil.* London: Tavistock.

Sabey, B. and Coding, P. (1975) 'Alcohol and road accidents in Great Britain'. In S. Israelstam and S. Lamber (eds) *Alcohol, Drugs and Road Safety.* Toronto: Addiction Research Foundation.

Sandler, J., Dare, C. and Holder, A. (1973) *The Patient and the Analyst.* London: George Allen and Unwin Ltd.

Saunders, W.M. (1984) 'Alcohol use in Britain: How much is too much?' *Health Education Journal 43*, 66–70.

The Brewer's Society (1992) *Statistical Handbook.* London: Arch Press.

White, A.C. (1980) 'Drinking and Accidents. A study of pre-accident drinking and total alcohol consumption in a sample of accident hospital patients'. In J.S. Madden, R. Walker and W.H. Kenyan (eds) *Aspects of Alcohol and Drug Dependence.* London: Pitman Medical.

Utne, H.E., Vallo Hansen, F., Winkler, K. and Schulsinger, F. (1977) 'Alcohol elimination rates in adoptees with and without alcoholic parents'. *Quarterly Journal of Studies on Alcohol 38*, 1219–1223.

Vaillant, G. (1983) *The Natural History of Alcoholism.* Cambridge Mass. and London: Harvard University Press.

Von Bertalanffy L. (1968) *General Systems Theory: Foundations, Development, Applications.* London: Allen Lane/The Penguin Press.

Further Reading and Information

General

Alcohol Concern (1991) *Warning: Alcohol can Damage your Health.* London: AC.

Alterman, A.I. (ed) (1985) *Kaufman in Substance Abuse and Psychopathology.* London: Plenum Press.

Anderson, P. (1989) *Alcohol Problems: A Practical Guide.* Oxford: Oxford University Press.

Arnold Ludwig (1988) *Understanding the Alcoholic's Mind: The Nature of Craving and How to Control it.* New York: Oxford University Press.

Chick, J. and Chick, J. (1984) *Drinking Problems – Information and Advice for the Individual, Family and Friends.* Edinburgh: Churchill Livingstone.

Coates, M. (1980) *Alcohol and Your Patient – A Nurses' Handbook.* Toronto: Toronto Addiction Research Foundation.

Collins, S. (ed) (1990) *Alcohol, Social Work and Helping.* London: Routledge.

Davies, I. and Raistrick, D. (1981) *Dealing with Drink.* London: British Broadcasting Corporation.

Denney, R.C. (1986) *Alcohol and Accidents.* Wilmslow: Sigma Press.

Edwards, G. (1988) 'As the years go rolling by', Lecture to Institute of Psychiatry. *British Journal of Psychiatry, 89.*

Edwards, G. and Grant, M. (1977) *Alcoholism – New Knowledge and New Responses.* London: Croom Helm.

Freddy, C. (1976) *The Alcohol Problem Explained.* Wellingborough, Northants: Thorsons Publishers.

Glass, I. (1991) *Addictive Behaviour.* London: Tavistock/Routledge.

Glatt, M.M. (1982) *Alcoholism.* Sevenoaks, Kent: Hodder and Stoughton.

Glatt, M.M. and Marks, J. (1982) *The Dependence Phenomenon.* London: MTP Press.

Goodwin, D. (1976) *Is Alcoholism Hereditary?* New York: Oxford University Press.

Grant, M. (1984) *Same Again – a Guide to Safer Drinking.* Harmondsworth: Penguin.

Grant, M. and Grinner, P.D.V. (eds) (1979) *Alcoholism in Perspective.* London, Croom Helm.

Grant, M., Plant, M. and Williams, A. (1983) *Economics and Alcohol.* London: Croom Helm.

Grant, M. and Ritson, B. (1983) *Alcohol – the Prevention Debate.* London: Croom Helm.

Hartz, C., Plant, M. and Watts, M. (1990) *Alcohol and Health – Handbook for Nurses, Midwives and Health Visitors.* London: Medical Council on Alcoholism.

Hore, B.D. and Ritson, M.D. (1986) *Alcohol and Health – A Handbook for Medical Students.* London: The Medical Council on Alcoholism.

Hunt, L. (1982) *Alcohol Related Problems.* London: Heinemann Educational Books.

Madden, J.S. (1979) *A Guide of Alcohol and Drug Dependence.* Bristol: John Wright and Sons Ltd.

Manson, L. (1990) *Alcohol and Health – a Handbook for Nurses, Midwives and Health Visitors.* London: Medical Council.

Maryon-Davis, A. (1989) *Pssst... The Really Useful Guide to Alcohol.* London: Pan.

Miller, W.K. (1976) 'Alcoholism Scales and Objective Assessment Methods – a Review'. *Psychological Bulletin, 83,* 649–674.

Miller, W.R.M. (ed) (1980) *The Addictive Behaviours.* Oxford: Pergamon.

Nolan, G. *et al.* (1988) *Alcohol and the Black Communities: Providing an Anti-Racist Service.* London: Dawn.

Orford, J. and Edwards, G. (1977) *Alcoholism.* Oxford: Oxford University Press.

Paton, A. (1988) *The ABC of Alcohol* (2nd edition) London: British Medical Association.

Pittman, D.C. and Synder, C.R. (1962) *Society, Culture and Drinking Patterns.* New York: John Wiley and Sons.

Prison Reform Trust (1989) *Drink, Delinquency and Prison*. London: Prison Reform Trust.

Richmond, F. and Dunne, N. (ed Sprince J) (1983) *It's Not Just Willpower...A Practical Guide to Working with Alcoholics*. Aylesbury, Bucks: Hazel Watson and Viney.

Robinson, D. (1976) *From Drinking to Alcoholism*. Chichester: John Wiley and Sons.

Robinson, J. (1989) *On the Demon Drink*. London: Methuen.

Rouerche, B. (1960) *The Neutral Spirit*. Boston: Little Brown and Co.

Royal College of General Practitioners (1986) *Alcohol: A Balanced View*. London: Royal College of General Practitioners.

Ruzek, J. and Vetter, C. (ed) (1973) *Drinkwatcher's Handbook*. Accept UK.

Shaw, S., Cartwright, A., Sprately, T. and Harwin, J. (1978) *Responding to Drinking Problems*. London: Croom Helm.

Solomon and Keeley (1982) *Perspectives in Drug and Alcohol Abuse – Similarities and Differences*. London: John Wright.

Steiner, C. (1971) *Games Alcoholics Play*. New York: Grove.

Stockwell, T. (1987) *Helping the Problem Drinker. New Initiatives in Community Care*. New York: Croom Helm.

Tether, P. and Robinson, D. (1986) *Preventing Alcohol Problems – A Guide to Local Action*. London: Tavistock Publications.

Webb, I. (1988) *Breaking the Habit*. London: Thames Television.

Wilkins, R. (1974) *The Hidden Alcoholic in General Practice*. London: Elek Science.

Valliant, G. (1983) *The Natural History of Alcoholism: Causes, Patterns and Paths to Recovery*. Boston, Massachusetts: Harvard University Press.

Family

Al-Anon Family Group Headquarters Inc. (1971) *The Dilemma of the Alcoholic Marriage*. New York: Al-Anon.

Jackson, J.K. (1954) 'The adjustment of the family to the cries of alcoholism'. *Quarterly Journal of Studies on Alcohol*, 15, 562–586.

Meyer, M.L. (1982) *Drinking Problems – Family Problems*. London: Momenta.

Meyer, M.L. (1982) *Drinking Problems – Family Problems* (practical guidelines for the problem drinker, the partner and all those involved) London: Momenta Publishing Ltd.

Orford, J. (1977) *A Comparison of Treatment and Advice, with a Study of the Influence of Marriage*. Oxford: Oxford University Press.

Pincus, L. and Dare, C. (19678) *Secrets in the Family*. London: Faber and Faber.

Walrond-Skinner, S. (1976) *The Family Therapy: Treatment of Natural Systems*. London: Routledge and Kegan Paul.

Wilson, M. (1989) *Living with a Drinker: How to Change Things*. London: Pandora.

Women

Camberwell Council on Alcoholism (1980) *Women, Alcohol*. London: Tavistock.

Corrigan, E.M. (1980) *Women in Treatment*. Oxford: Oxford University Press.

Kent, R. (1989) *Say When! Everything a Woman Needs to Know About Alcohol*. London: Sheldon Press.

McConville, Brigid (1991) *Women Under the Influence: Alcohol and its Impact*. London: Grafton.

Plant, M. (1985) *Women, Drinking and Pregnancy*. London: Tavistock.

Pratt, O. (1981) 'Alcohol and the woman of childbearing age: a public health problem'. *British Journal of Addiction*, 353–390.

Roth, P. (1991) *Alcohol and Drugs are Women's Issues – a Review of the Issues*. London: Scarecrow Press.

Young People

British Medical Association (1986) *Young People and Alcohol*. London: BMA

Hawker, A. (1978) *Adolescents and Alcohol*. London: Edsall.

O'Connor, J. (1978) *The Young Drinkers*. London: Tavistock.

Scott, J. (1992) *Alcohol and HIV AIDS: Report of Research into the Role of Alcohol and Unsafe Sexual Behaviour*. Allington: NHS.

Young People and Alcohol – Report of Board of Science and Education (1986) London: British Medical Association.

Medical

Drummond, D., Thom, B., Brown, C., Edwards, G. and Mullan, M. (1990) *Specialist Versus General Practioner Treatment of Problem Drinkers*. The Lancet. October. 336 pp.915–918.

Gross, M.M. (ed) (1973) *Alcohol Intoxication and Withdrawal*. New York: Plenum.

Mason, P. and Fitch, V. (1991) 'Promoting safer drinking in general practice'. *Health Education Journal* 50. No 4. 204–207.

Richter, D. (1980) *Addiction and Brain Damage*. London: Croom Helm.

Royal College of Psychiatrists (1986) *Alcohol: Our Favorite Drug*. London: Tavistock.

Sprott, M.V. (1992) *Alcohol Tolerance and Drinking: Learning the Consequences*. New York: Guilford Publications.

Wilkins, R.H. (1974) *The Hidden Alcoholic in General Practice*. London: Elek Science.

The Workplace

Dickenson, F. (1988) *Drink and Drugs at Work*. London: Institute of Personnel Management.

Doogan, K. and Means, P. (1990) *Alcohol and the Workplace*. Bristol: University of Bristol S.C.

Grant, M. *et al*. (1977) *Alcoholism and Industry*. AEC/MLCCA.

Hore, B.D. and Plant, M.A. (1981) *Alcohol Problems in Employment*. London: Croom Helm.

Schramm, G.J. (ed) (1971) *Alcoholism and its Treatment in Industry*. Baltimore: John Hopkins University Press.

Psychological Approaches

Bean, M.H. and Zimberg, N.E. (eds) (1981) *Dynamic Approaches to the Understanding and Treatment of Alcoholism*. New York: Free Press.

Bowlby, J. (1973) *Separation*. Harmondsworth: Penguin.

Blane, H. (1968) *The Personality of the Alcoholic Guises of Dependency*. Canada: Harper and Rowe.

Culley, S. (1991) *Integrative Counselling Skills in Action*. London: Sage.

Davidson, R., Dollnick, S. and MacEwan, I. (1991) *Counselling Problem Drinkers*. London: Routledge.

Jacobs, M. (1988) *Psychodynamic Counselling in Action*. London: Sage.

Knight, R.P. (1937) 'The psychodynamics of chronic alcoholism'. *Journal of Nervous and Mental Diseases*. Chapter 86 538–548.

Rycroft, C. (1968) *Anxiety Neurosis*. Harmondsworth: Penguin.

Homelessness

Cook, T. (1975) *Vagrant Alcoholics*. Boston: Routledge and Kegan Paul.

Greater Manchester and Liverpool Council on Alcoholism (1986) *Alcohol and Homelessness*. GMLCA.

Otto, S. and Orford, J. (1978) *Not Quite Like Home: Small Hostels for Alcoholics and Others.* Chichester: John Wiley and Sons.

Drinking and Driving

Department of Environment (1976) *Drinking and Driving.* London: HMSO.

Medical Commission on Accident Prevention (1974) *Medical Aspects of Fitness to Drive.* A guide for medical practitioners.

Old Age

Barnes, G.M. (1980) *Alcohol and the Elderly: A Comprehensive Bibliography.* Westport, CT: Greenwood Press.

Goodman, C. and Ward, M. (1989) *Alcohol Problems in Old Age.* London: Staccato Books and Training.

Leaflets

That's the Limit: Health Education Authority.

Black Women and Alcohol – an information booklet: DAWN.

Guide to Alcohol and Accidents: BMA (1988).

BMA (1988) The Drinking Driver: BMA.

Sabey, B. (1988) *Drinking and Driving – the Road Ahead.* Aquarius

Alcohol Concern (1988) *Drinkwise 1987 Evaluation.* Alcohol Concern.

Alcohol Concern (1988) *Drinkwise: A Manual or Local Campaigners.* Alcohol Concern.

Alcohol Concern (1991) *Alcohol Education: A Practical Handbook or Occasional Teachers.* Alcohol Concern.

Good Practices in Mental Health (1986) *Alcohol Services Information Pack.* Good Practices in Mental Health/Alcohol Concern.

Grant, M. (1980) *Alcohol Education for Young People in Scotland.* AEC.

National Council on Alcoholism, UK (1981) *Counsellors' Guide on Problem Drinking.* London, National Council on Alcoholism.

Alcoholics Anonymous (1977) *Twelve Steps and Twelve Traditions.* New York: Alcoholics Anonymous World Services.

AIDS (1987) *What Everyone Needs to Know.* Health Education Authority.

The Facts about Drinking and Driving: Transport and Road Research Laboratory.

Problem Drinker in the Family? – a guide for dealing with drinking problems: Alcohol Counselling and Information Service.

A DIY Guide to Sensible Drinking for Young People: Alcohol Advisory Centre.

Over 60? – A DIY Guide to Sensible Drinking for the Over 60's: Alcohol Advisory Centre.

Alcohol and Older People – Safer Drinking for the Over 60's – A guide for family, relatives and friends: Alcohol Concern in association with Age Concern (1988).

Sensible Drinking – Here's How: Drink Wisely Northwest.

Ward, M. Helping Problem Drinkers – A Practical Guide for the Caring Professions: Kent Council on Addiction.

Alateen – Is it for You?: Al-Anon Family Groups UK and Eire.

Women's Health Matters: National Union of Public Employees.

Useful Addresses and Telephone Numbers

Health Education Authority
Hamilton House
Mabledon Place
London WC1H 9BD
Tel: (071) 631 0930

Alcohol Counselling and Information Service
24 Hazlewood Road
Northampton NN1 1LN
Tel: Northampton (0604) 22121

Alcohol Advisory Centre
14 Park Row
Bristol BS1 5LJ
Tel: Bristol (0272) 293028/9

Age Concern England
60 Pitcairn Road
Mitcham
Surrey CR4 3LL
Tel: (081) 640 5431

Alcohol Concern
305 Gray's Inn Road
London WC1X 8QF
Tel: (071) 833 3471

Alcohol Concern Wales
24 Park Place
Cardiff CF1 3BA
Tel: (0222) 398791/378855

Scottish Council on Alcohol
137–145 Sauchiehall Street
Glasgow G2 3EW
Tel: (041) 333 9677

Northern Ireland Council on Alcohol
40 Elmwood Avenue
Belfast BT9 6AZ
Tel: (0232) 664434

Accept Services UK
200 Seagrave Road
London SW6 1RQ
Tel: (071) 381 3157

Alcoholics Anonymous
Head Office
General Service Office
PO Box 1
Stonebow House
York YO1 2NJ
Tel: (0904) 352 644026
London: (071) 352 3001
Scotland: (041) 221 9027
Northern Ireland:
(0232) 681084
Wales South West:
(0222) 373771
Wales West: (09945) 282

Al-Anon and Alateen
London: (071) 403 0888
(24 hour)
Belfast: (0232) 243489
Glasgow: (041) 221 7356

Libra Project
Oxford Council on Alcohol and Drug Use
1 Tidmarsh Lane
Oxford OX1 1NG
Tel: Oxford (0865) 244447

Medical Council on Alcoholism
1 St. Andrew's Place
London NW1 4LB
Tel: (071) 487 4445

Al-Anon Family Groups UK and Eire
61 Great Dover Street
London SE1 4YF
Tel: (071) 403 0888 (24 hour)

Institute of Alcohol Studies
Alliance House
12 Caxton Street
London SW1 0QS
Tel: (071) 222 4001/5880

CADD – Campaign Against Drink Driving
Meadside, Shudy Camps
Cambridge CB1 6RA
Tel: (079) 984 645

CCOAD – The Churches Council on Alcohol and Drugs
4 Southampton Row
London WC1B 4AA
Tel: (071) 242 6511

DAWN – Drugs, Women, Alcohol, Nationally
Omnibus Workspace
39 North Road
London N7 9DP
Tel: (071) 700 4653

Drinkwatchers
c/o ACCEPT Clinic
200 Seagrave Road
London SW6 1RQ
Tel: (071) 381 3155

RoSPA – The Royal Society for the Prevention of Accidents
Cannon House
The Prior
Queensway
Birmingham B4 6BS
Tel: (021) 200 1254

Women's Alcohol Centre
254 St. Paul's Road
London N1
Tel: (071) 226 4581

Subject Index

Name Index